# MOLDAVITE

## The Gren Stone

Moldavite

The Green Stone

Blue Dragoon Books

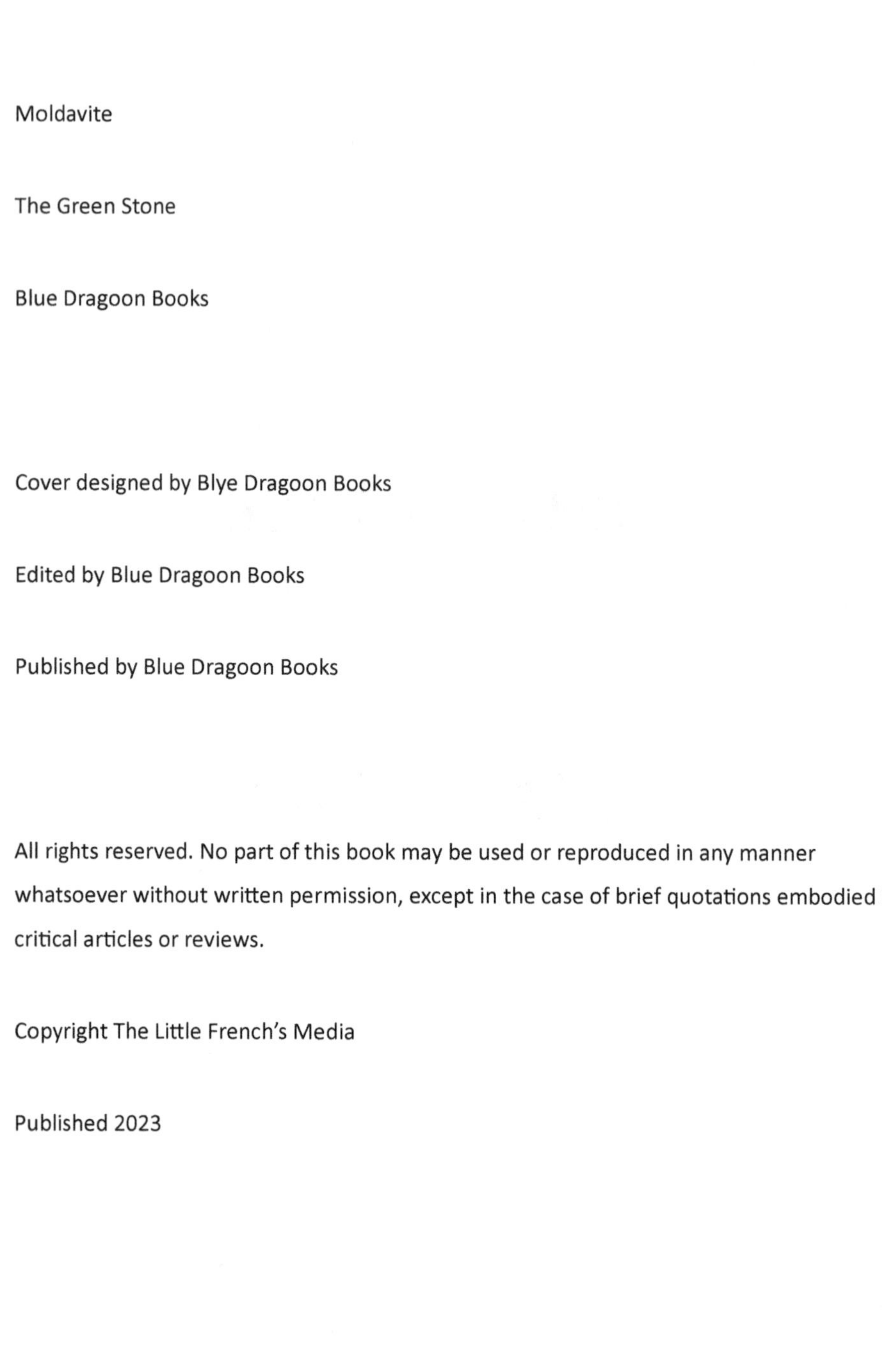

Cover designed by Blye Dragoon Books

Edited by Blue Dragoon Books

Published by Blue Dragoon Books





Published 2023

# CHAPTER 1

"MOLDAVITE" GREEN STONE

"The gem that fell from the sky"

Moldavite is a beautiful green stone that has been valued by humans for thousands of years. It is the only gem that is known to have fallen from the sky as a result of a meteorite impact. Moldavite is said to have many powerful spiritual and healing properties.

In the Neolithic period, Moldavite was used to make arrowheads, cutting tools, and amulets. It was also believed to have spiritual powers. Archaeologists have found Moldavite at the site of the Venus of Willendorf, a famous Neolithic statuette. The Venus of Willendorf is a voluptuous female figure that is thought to be a symbol of fertility. The presence of Moldavite at this site suggests that it was seen as a sacred stone.

Moldavite is still used today in jewelry and other decorative objects. It is also said to be a powerful healing tool. Moldavite is believed to promote spiritual growth, emotional healing, and physical well-being. It is also said to be helpful for manifesting desires.

Moldavite is a unique and special stone. It is a gift from the cosmos that has been cherished by humans for thousands of years. If you are lucky enough to own a piece of Moldavite, cherish it and use its energy to create positive change in your life.

The figure of this naked woman (Venus of Willendorf) (figures N ° 1-01), is 11.1 cm high with 15 cm of width and shape plump, was sculpted in monolithic limestone, which is not in the region, and painted with ochre.

Figure 1-01

The Venus of Willendorf is a fascinating artifact that has been the subject of much speculation and debate. Its unusual anatomical features have led scholars to believe that it is a symbol of fertility. The sculpture's lack of visible facial features and its covered head have also been interpreted in various ways. Some believe that the hairstyle represents braids, a hood, or a veil. Others believe that the absence of facial features is intentional and represents the universality of the female form.

The folklore of the Czech Republic associates Moldavite with harmony, perseverance, and conjugal relations. It is often given as a wedding gift to symbolize the hope of a happy and fruitful marriage. Moldavite is also said to have healing properties. In some legends, the Holy Grail is said to be made of Moldavite. This association may be due to the stone's otherworldly origins and its purported spiritual powers.

The legend of the Holy Grail has been interpreted in many different ways. Some believe that it is a physical object, such as a cup or a stone. Others believe that it is a symbol of spiritual enlightenment or divine grace. The Holy Grail is often associated with the quest for meaning and purpose in life.

The connection between the Venus of Willendorf, Moldavite, and the Holy Grail is a fascinating one. It suggests that these objects have been imbued with symbolic meaning for thousands of years. They represent the human desire for fertility, healing, and spiritual connection. As we continue to explore the mysteries of the past, we may gain a deeper understanding of the significance of these ancient artifacts.

Moldavite is a powerful healing stone that can help us to achieve harmony, well-being, and spiritual connection. It is said to be a gift from the cosmos and a harbinger of a better future for humanity. However, it is important to be aware of the possibility of fraud when purchasing Moldavite. There are many unscrupulous individuals who try to sell fake Moldavite to unsuspecting buyers.

Here are a few tips for identifying genuine Moldavite:

- Moldavite is always green in color. It can range from a light olive green to a deep bottle green.

- Moldavite has a unique texture that is often described as "glassy" or "waxy." It is also often pitted or bubbly.

- Moldavite is slightly radioactive. If you have a Geiger counter, you can use it to test the radioactivity of a Moldavite stone.

- Moldavite is relatively rare. If you are offered a piece of Moldavite at a very low price, it is likely to be fake.

- It is always best to purchase Moldavite from a reputable dealer.

The story of Napoleon and the fake Holy Grail is a reminder that even the most powerful people can be fooled by clever imposters. It is important to be vigilant and to do your research before making any purchases of valuable objects.

The hex Genoa vessel known as the Sacro Catino is another example of a religious artifact that has been the subject of controversy. The Sacro Catino is a green glass dish that was once believed to be the Holy Grail. However, it has since been determined to be a medieval hoax.

The stories of the fake Holy Grail and the Sacro Catino are a warning about the dangers of credulity. We should always be critical of claims that seem too good to be true. We should also be wary of people who try to pressure us into making quick decisions. By doing our research and using our common sense, we can protect ourselves from being deceived.

The Sacro Catino is a fascinating artifact with a rich and complex history. It is a green glass dish that was once believed to be the Holy Grail. The dish is 37 centimeters in diameter and is thought to have been made in Egypt.

The origin of the Sacro Catino is uncertain. According to one account, it was found in the mosque of Caesarea in 1101 by the Genoese during the First Crusade. The Genoese believed that it was made of emerald and accepted it as payment for their services. Another account claims that the dish was found by Alfonso VII of Castile when he captured the castle of Almeria in 1147 with the help of the Genoese.

The identification of the Sacro Catino with the Holy Grail was made by Jacobus of Voragine in his Chronicle of Genoa, written in the late 13th century. Voragine claimed that the dish had been used by Jesus Christ at the Last Supper. This legend made the Sacro Catino a highly revered object in Genoa.

The Sacro Catino was taken to Paris by Napoleon in 1797. It was returned to Genoa in 1815, but it was broken in the process. The broken dish is now on display in the Treasure Museum of St. Lorenzo Cathedral in Genoa.

The Sacro Catino is a reminder of the enduring power of myth and legend. The belief that it was the Holy Grail made it a potent symbol of religious faith. The dish's story is also a testament to the human desire to find meaning in the world. We often look for objects or symbols that represent our deepest hopes and aspirations. The Sacro Catino is one example of such an object.

The Sacro Catino is a fascinating artifact with a long and complex history. It is a symbol of faith, myth, and legend. The dish's story is a reminder of the power of human imagination.

## The Moldavite Chalice and the Lost Kingdom of Shambhala

In the tapestry of history, a golden chalice, adorned with enigmatic moldavite stones, emerges as a beacon of mystery. This chalice, revered throughout the ages, vanished during the tumultuous years of World War II, leaving behind a trail of unanswered questions. Its whereabouts remain a tantalizing enigma, shrouded in whispers of its otherworldly origins.

Nicholas Roerich, the visionary Russian artist and explorer, was drawn to the enigmatic allure of the Moldavite Chalice. Driven by a deep spiritual calling, he embarked on a quest to uncover the secrets of Shambhala, the legendary kingdom said to be hidden within the snow-capped peaks of the Himalayas. Roerich believed that the chalice was inextricably linked to this mystical realm, holding the key to unlocking its ancient wisdom.

In the 1920s and 1930s, Roerich and his wife, Helena, embarked on a series of arduous expeditions to the Himalayas, traversing through treacherous landscapes and seeking clues about the lost kingdom. Along their journey, they encountered Tibetan monks and lamas, who shared with them their knowledge of Shambhala and its profound significance.

Roerich's unwavering belief in the Agni Mani, the mystical moldavite stone in his possession, fueled his determination to find Shambhala. He believed that the stone was a sacred relic entrusted to him by the King of Shambhala, a benevolent being who oversaw humanity's spiritual evolution. Roerich felt a profound responsibility to return the Agni Mani to its rightful place, believing that it held the power to transform the world.

Despite the challenges he faced, Roerich never wavered in his pursuit of Shambhala. His paintings, infused with the ethereal beauty of the Himalayas and the spiritual quest that consumed him, became a testament to his unwavering faith. His writings and lectures further illuminated the mysteries of Shambhala, sparking a global fascination with this elusive realm.

The Moldavite Chalice, imbued with an otherworldly energy, remains a symbol of hope and spiritual awakening. Its existence, whether physical or ethereal, represents the enduring human desire to seek the hidden truths that lie beyond the veil of the ordinary. It is a reminder of the power of faith, the allure of the unknown, and the unwavering quest for enlightenment.

While the chalice's physical fate remains uncertain, its legacy lives on in the hearts and minds of those who continue to search for Shambhala. The chalice has become a potent symbol of spiritual transformation, reminding us that even in the darkest of times, the light of hope and enlightenment can never be extinguished.

As we embark on our own journeys of self-discovery, let us remember the Moldavite Chalice and the wisdom it represents. May it inspire us to delve deeper into the mysteries of life, to seek the hidden truths that lie within us, and to strive towards a brighter future for all.

# CHAPTER 2

ORIGIN OF THE GREEN STONE "MOLDAVITE

"The gem that fell from the sky"

## The Mystery of Moldavite's Origin

The origin of moldavite, a rare green gemstone, has been a subject of debate and speculation for centuries. Its unique properties and enigmatic appearance have led to the development of numerous theories about its formation.

One hypothesis suggests that moldavite is of extraterrestrial origin. This theory is supported by the stone's high silica content and its association with meteorite impact craters in the Czech Republic. According to this theory, moldavite was formed when a meteorite impacted Earth, melting and vaporizing the surrounding rocks. The vaporized material then condensed and rained back down to Earth, forming moldavite deposits.

Another hypothesis suggests that moldavite is terrestrial in origin. This theory proposes that moldavite was formed by the impact of a meteorite or comet, or by volcanic activity. The impact or volcanic event would have melted and vaporized Earth's crust, creating moldavite as a byproduct.

A third hypothesis suggests that moldavite is a combination of terrestrial and extraterrestrial materials. According to this theory, moldavite was formed when a meteorite or comet impacted Earth, melting and mixing with Earth's crust. The resulting mixture would have solidified to form moldavite.

Scientists are still working to determine the true origin of moldavite. However, the following evidence suggests that moldavite is extraterrestrial in origin:

**Moldavite** is found in association with meteorite impact craters.

**Moldavite** has a high silica content, similar to tektites, which are known to be extraterrestrial in origin.

**Moldavite** has a unique chemical composition that is not found in any known terrestrial rocks.

**Moldavite** has a high concentration of rare earth elements, which are also found in tektites.

The discovery of moldavite in meteorites and other extraterrestrial objects further supports the extraterrestrial origin hypothesis. In 2019, scientists discovered moldavite in a meteorite that fell in Australia. This discovery provides direct evidence that moldavite can form in extraterrestrial environments.

The mystery of moldavite's origin is likely to continue for some time. However, the evidence suggests that moldavite is a rare and unique gemstone with an extraterrestrial origin. Its formation is a testament to the power of cosmic collisions and the mysteries of the universe.

### Moldavite: A Stone of Healing and Transformation

Moldavite is a powerful green gemstone that has been revered for its healing and transformative properties. It is a relatively rare stone, found only in a few locations around the world. Moldavite is thought to have formed from the impact of a meteorite on Earth, and its unique properties are attributed to its extraterrestrial origins.

- **Healing Properties:** Moldavite is said to be a powerful healing stone for both the physical and emotional body. It is believed to cleanse and purify the aura, promote emotional balance, and stimulate the body's natural healing processes. Moldavite is also said to be effective for pain relief, reducing stress, and boosting the immune system.

- **Transformative Properties:** Moldavite is known as a stone of transformation. It is believed to help people awaken to their true potential and make positive changes in their lives. Moldavite can help people to release limiting beliefs, clear negative karma, and open up to new possibilities. It can also help people to connect with their spiritual selves and find their true purpose in life.

- **Selective and Powerful:** Moldavite is a selective stone. It does not respond to everyone in the same way. It is drawn to those who are ready for change and transformation. Moldavite can be a powerful force for good, but it can also be challenging to work with. It is important to use moldavite with respect and intention.

- **Fractal Nature:** Moldavite is a fractal stone. This means that each small fragment of moldavite has the same properties as the whole stone. This makes moldavite a very versatile stone that can be used in many different ways.

- **Source of Light:** Moldavite is said to be a source of light. It is believed to amplify the energy of other stones and to help people to connect with higher dimensions of consciousness. Moldavite can be used to create a sacred space for meditation, prayer, or healing.

The green stone "Moldavite" is a gift from the universe. It is a powerful tool for healing, transformation, and spiritual growth. It is important to use moldavite with respect and intention. When used correctly, moldavite can help to create a more beautiful and harmonious world.

# The Location of Moldavite Deposits

Moldavite is a rare green gemstone that is found in only a few places around the world. The majority of moldavite deposits are located in the Czech Republic, in the region of Bohemia. Moldavite is also found in small amounts in Slovakia, Germany, and Austria.

**Czech Republic:** The Czech Republic is the most significant source of moldavite. Moldavite deposits are found in a region of southern Bohemia known as the Moldavite Belt. The Moldavite Belt is an area of about 23,000 square kilometers that was impacted by a meteorite shower approximately 15 million years ago. The impact created a series of craters and scattered moldavite across the landscape.

**Slovakia:** Moldavite deposits are also found in Slovakia, in the regions of Moravia and Silesia. The Slovakian moldavite is similar in appearance to the Czech moldavite, but it is often smaller in size.

**Germany:** Moldavite has been found in a few locations in Germany, including the states of Bavaria and Saxony. The

German moldavite is typically darker in color than the Czech and Slovakian moldavite.

**Austria:** Moldavite has also been found in a few locations in Austria, including the states of Lower Austria and Upper Austria. The Austrian moldavite is similar in appearance to the German moldavite.

In recent years, moldavite has also been found in Venezuela. In 2019, a meteorite of moldavite was discovered in the Guyana Highlands, in the southern part of the country. The Venezuelan moldavite is similar in appearance to the Czech moldavite.

The discovery of moldavite in Venezuela is significant because it suggests that moldavite may be found in other parts of the world. It is possible that moldavite deposits have been overlooked or misidentified in other regions. As scientists continue to search for moldavite, they may discover new deposits in unexpected locations.

The location of moldavite deposits is a complex topic. The formation of moldavite is still not fully understood. However, it is believed that moldavite was formed by the impact of a meteorite on Earth. The impact melted and vaporized the Earth's crust, creating moldavite as a byproduct. The moldavite was then scattered across the landscape by the impact blast.

The exact location of moldavite deposits is determined by a number of factors, including the size and direction of the meteorite impact, the type of rocks that were present at the impact site, and the subsequent erosion and weathering of the landscape. Moldavite deposits are often found in areas with exposed bedrock, such as riverbeds, cliffs, and quarries.

The search for moldavite deposits is a challenging but rewarding task. Moldavite is a rare gemstone, and its deposits are often small and difficult to find. However, the discovery of a new moldavite deposit can be a significant event. Moldavite is a valuable gemstone, and it is also a source of scientific interest.

In the Guyana Highlands of Venezuela, a remarkable discovery has been made: a meteorite of green moldavite. This meteorite is significant for several reasons:

It is the first large moldavite meteorite ever found. Most moldavite is found in small pieces, typically weighing a few grams or less. This meteorite, however, is estimated to have weighed over 300 kilograms before it was broken during extraction.

It is located in a new location. Moldavite is typically found in the Czech Republic, Slovakia, Germany, and Austria. The discovery of moldavite in Venezuela suggests that it may be found in other parts of the world as well.

It provides insights into the formation of moldavite. The meteorite is well-preserved, allowing scientists to study its composition and structure in detail. This information may help to shed light on the process by which moldavite is formed.

The meteorite is believed to have fallen to Earth approximately 15 million years ago. It is thought to have been part of a larger meteorite shower that impacted the Earth in the area now known as the Czech Republic. The impact caused the meteorite to break into pieces, which were scattered across the area. Some of these pieces were transported to Venezuela by glaciers or rivers.

The green moldavite meteorite is composed of a unique type of glass that is not found anywhere else on Earth. This glass is thought to have formed when the meteorite impacted the Earth. The impact melted and vaporized the surrounding rocks, creating a molten cloud of material. This cloud then cooled and solidified to form moldavite.

The meteorite is a valuable source of scientific information. Scientists are studying the meteorite to learn more about its composition, structure, and origin. They are also interested in the possibility that moldavite may have unique properties that could be used in new technologies.

The discovery of the green moldavite meteorite is a significant event in the field of geology. It is a reminder that the Earth is constantly being bombarded by objects from space. These impacts can have a profound impact on the planet, both in the short-term and the long-term. The study of meteorites helps us to understand the history of the Earth and the processes that have shaped it.

The green moldavite meteorite is also a beautiful and unique object. It is a reminder of the power and mystery of the cosmos. The meteorite is a testament to the interconnectedness of all things in the universe. It is a reminder that we are all part of something larger than ourselves.

The green moldavite meteorite found in Venezuela is a fascinating object. The observation that moldavite has penetrated into fissures or cracks in the meteorite is significant. This suggests that moldavite was molten when it impacted the Earth. The molten moldavite would have flowed into any cracks or fissures that were present in the meteorite.

The fact that moldavite is found in the front section of the meteorite is also significant. This is the part of the meteorite that would have experienced the most intense heating during impact. The high temperatures would have melted the moldavite, allowing it to flow into the cracks and fissures.

The observation that moldavite has penetrated into the meteorite is evidence that the moldavite was formed during the impact event. This supports the hypothesis that moldavite is formed when a meteorite impacts the Earth. The impact melts and vaporizes the surrounding rocks, creating a molten cloud of material. This cloud then cools and solidifies to form moldavite.

The study of the green moldavite meteorite is providing valuable insights into the formation of moldavite. The meteorite is a well-preserved example of an impact crater, and the moldavite that is found within the crater provides important evidence about the impact process. Scientists are using this information to better understand how moldavite is formed and how it relates to other types of impact glass.

The research on the green moldavite meteorite is ongoing. Scientists are continuing to study the meteorite to learn more about its composition, structure, and origin. They are also interested in the possibility that moldavite may have unique properties that could be used in new technologies. The meteorite is a valuable resource for scientific research, and it is helping us to better understand the processes that have shaped our planet.

The green moldavite meteorite is a complex and fascinating object. The different parts of the meteorite exhibit different features, depending on the temperature and conditions they experienced during the impact event.

**Front section:** The front section of the meteorite is the part that experienced the most intense heating during impact. The moldavite in this section is molten and has penetrated into fissures and cracks in the meteorite.

**Side and rear sections:** The side and rear sections of the meteorite were exposed to lower temperatures during impact. The moldavite in these sections may be fused with sand from the ground. The degree of fusion depends on the temperature of the meteorite and the composition of the sand.

**Intact samples:** Some samples of moldavite from the meteorite are completely intact. These samples have not been altered by fusion or weathering. They provide valuable insights into the original composition and structure of the meteorite.

**Jewelry-quality stones:** Many of the moldavite samples from the meteorite are of jewelry quality. They are clear, transparent, and have a beautiful green color. These stones are highly sought-after by collectors and jewelers.

**Stones with inclusions:** Some of the moldavite samples from the meteorite contain inclusions of other minerals. These inclusions can be sand, dust, or even small pieces of the original meteorite. The inclusions add to the unique character of the stones.

**Incomplete collection:** The meteorite has not yet been fully collected. There are likely more moldavite samples in the area. The discovery of additional samples could provide even more information about the meteorite and its formation.

The green moldavite meteorite is a valuable scientific resource. It is providing scientists with new insights into the formation of moldavite and the impact process. The meteorite is also a beautiful and unique object. The different parts of the meteorite exhibit a variety of features, each of which tells a story about the meteorite's journey through space and its impact on Earth.

## Conclusion on The Origin of The "Moldavite" Green Stone

The authors' conclusion that the green moldavite stone is a meteorite from outer space is supported by the following evidence:

- The stones have unique characteristics and special properties that are not found in any terrestrial rocks. Moldavite is a natural glass that has a characteristic green color and a smooth, etched surface. It is also highly magnetic and has a high electrical conductivity. These properties are not found in any rocks that are known to have originated on Earth.

- The stones were found in a concentrated area, suggesting that they originated from a single event. Moldavite is found in a relatively small area of Central Europe, including the Czech Republic, Slovakia, Germany, and Austria. This suggests that the moldavite stones were all created by the same event, such as a meteorite impact.

- The stones are similar in composition to tektites, which are known to be formed by meteorite impacts. Tektites are natural glasses that are formed when a meteorite impacts the Earth's surface. The composition of moldavite is very similar to that of tektites, suggesting that moldavite was also formed by a meteorite impact.

- The theory that moldavite is from the Orion constellation is no longer supported by scientific evidence. The Orion constellation is located in a different part of the sky than the region where moldavite is found. Additionally, the stars in the Orion constellation are not close enough together to be considered a system.

- The Sirius stars are a more likely source of moldavite, as they form a true system of three stars. The Sirius stars are located in the Canis Major constellation, which is relatively close to the region where moldavite is found. The Sirius stars are also arranged in a system, which could explain why moldavite stones are often found in clusters.

The authors' conclusion is further supported by the fact that moldavite stones from Moldova and Venezuela have similar properties. This suggests that moldavite is a global phenomenon, rather than being confined to a specific region.

Overall, the evidence strongly suggests that the green moldavite stone is a meteorite from outer space. The authors' research has made a significant contribution to our understanding of the origin of moldavite. Their findings are likely to be of interest to scientists, collectors, and anyone else who is fascinated by these mysterious stones.

The authors here are making a bold claim: that the green moldavite stone originated from the Sirius star system. They support their claim with the following evidence:

- The Sirius star system is a triple star system. This means that it consists of three stars that orbit each other. The authors believe that this is significant because ancient writings often mention moldavite as being associated with three stars.

- The Sirius star system is relatively close to Earth. It is located only 8.6 light-years away. This means that it is close enough for moldavite to have been ejected from the system and traveled to Earth.

- The Sirius star system is young. It is only about 200 million years old. This means that it is possible that moldavite was ejected from the system during its formation.

- The composition of moldavite is similar to that of tektites. Tektites are natural glasses that are formed when a meteorite impacts Earth. This suggests that moldavite may have been formed in a similar way.

- The authors have found moldavite stones that are similar in appearance to those found in Moldova. This suggests that the moldavite stones from both locations may have a common origin.

The authors' claim is a significant one. If it is correct, it would mean that moldavite is a gift from the stars. This would be a remarkable discovery that would change our understanding of the universe.

The authors' evidence is compelling, but it is important to note that it is not definitive. There are other possible explanations for the origin of moldavite. For example, it is possible that moldavite was formed by a volcanic eruption on Earth.

More research is needed to confirm the authors' claim. However, their work has made an important contribution to our understanding of the origin of moldavite. I am excited to see what future research reveals about this mysterious stone.

Moldavite is a very rare stone, much rarer than diamonds. It is estimated that only about 1500 kilograms of Moldavite have been collected in the world since prehistoric times. The largest deposits of Moldavite are found in the Czech Republic, with smaller deposits in Austria and Germany. The most famous deposits are in the Besednice, Locenice, Slavce, and Chlum areas.

Moldavite is believed to have formed when a meteorite impacted the Earth about 15 million years ago. The impact melted the ground and ejected molten material into the atmosphere, where it cooled and solidified into tektites. Tektites are natural glasses that are formed from meteorite impacts.

The map you have inserted shows the landmass that existed on Earth during the late Miocene epoch, when the Moldavite meteorite is believed to have impacted. The only landmass in that area was to the north of the current Alps, which is consistent with the known distribution of Moldavite deposits.

So, to answer your question, yes, Moldavite is a very rare stone that is found in only a few places in the world. It is believed to have formed from a meteorite impact, and the only landmass that existed in the area at the time of the impact was to the north of the current Alps.

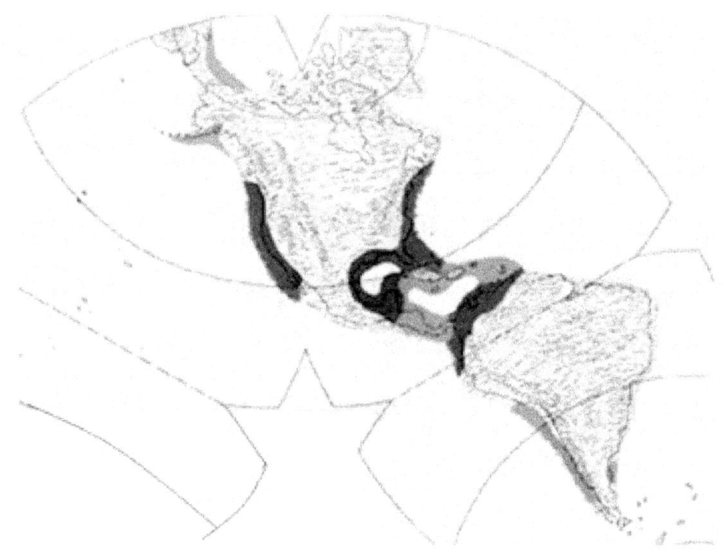

The map you have shows that the Americas were already well-defined by the late Miocene epoch, so it is possible that meteorites could have impacted in other parts of the continent. In fact, there have been a few meteorites found in North America that are thought to be of the same age as the Moldavite meteorite. For example, the Willamette meteorite is a large tektite that was found in Oregon, and it is thought to have fallen to Earth about 15 million years ago.

So, it is certainly possible that other meteorites of the same age as Moldavite could be found in other parts of the Americas. However, it is also possible that they have already been eroded or buried by sediment. Only further research will tell for sure.

In the meantime, it is interesting to consider the possibility that these meteorites could have had a significant impact on the evolution of life on Earth. For example, the impact of the Moldavite meteorite may have caused a mass extinction event, clearing the way for the evolution of new species. Or the impact of another meteorite may have helped to spread life from one continent to another.

The possibilities are endless, and it is one of the things that makes the study of meteorites so fascinating.

## "Moldavite" Green Stone in The Eastern Hemisphere

The area where Moldavite is found today is not the same place where it originally fell. The meteorite that created Moldavite is believed to have impacted in the Nördlinger Ries crater in Germany, which is about 450 kilometers away from the Moldau River Valley in the Czech Republic. The impact melted the ground and ejected molten material into the atmosphere, where it cooled and solidified into tektites. The tektites were then transported by wind and water to the Moldau River Valley, where they were deposited.

It is possible that other meteorites of the same age as Moldavite could have impacted other parts of the world, but there is no evidence to support this claim. The only known deposits of Moldavite are in the Czech Republic, Austria, and Germany.

The map you have shows that the Americas were already well-defined by the late Miocene epoch, so it is possible that meteorites could have impacted in other parts of the continent. However, it is also possible that they have already been eroded or buried by sediment. Only further research will tell for sure.

It is certainly an interesting idea to consider the possibility that other meteorites of the same age as Moldavite could be found in other parts of the Americas. However, it is also important to be realistic about the chances of finding them. The Moldavite deposits are very well-known and have been studied for centuries. If there were other deposits of Moldavite in the Americas, they would likely have been found by now.

So, while it is possible that other meteorites of the same age as Moldavite could be found in the Americas, it is also possible that they do not exist. Only further research will tell for sure.

The meteorite is believed to have impacted in the Nördlinger Ries crater in Germany, and the Moldavite was then transported to the Moldau River Valley by wind and water.

The oldest sediments where Moldavite has been found are associated with sands and clays of river alluvium. This suggests that the Moldavite was transported to these areas by rivers. The fact that the Moldavite is found in such a narrow area also suggests that it was transported by a relatively short distance.

**The Czech Republic**

The deposits of Moldavite in the Czech Republic are divided into two main types: primary and secondary. Primary deposits are those that are found in the immediate vicinity of the impact site. Secondary deposits are those that are found further away from the impact site, and they are thought to have been transported by rivers or glaciers.

**Besednice**

The most famous primary deposit of Moldavite is the Besednice deposit. This deposit is located in the Bohemian Forest, about 40 kilometers from the Nördlinger Ries crater. The Besednice deposit is the largest and most productive deposit of Moldavite in the world.

**Chlum-Skalice**

The most famous secondary deposit of Moldavite is the Chlum-Skalice deposit. This deposit is located in the Central Bohemian Uplands, about 100 kilometers from the Nördlinger Ries crater. The Chlum-Skalice deposit is the second largest deposit of Moldavite in the world.

There are also a number of smaller deposits of Moldavite scattered throughout the Czech Republic. These deposits are typically found in river gravel or in clays.

The study of Moldavite deposits is a fascinating area of research. It can tell us a lot about the history of the Earth and the evolution of life. It can also help us to understand the formation of tektites and the impact of meteorites on Earth.

## South Bohemia

This is the largest area where Moldavite is found. The area covers an area of 2000 square kilometers, and there are about seventy (70) known deposits of Moldavite in the region.

The characteristics of the Moldavites in this area vary depending on the location where they are found. The oldest Moldavites in South Bohemia are found in the Middle Miocene period, in formations of sand and gravel. These Moldavites are typically smaller and less well-formed than the Moldavites that are found in younger sediments.

The younger Moldavites in South Bohemia are found in river and lake sediments. These Moldavites are typically larger and more well-formed than the older Moldavites. They are also more likely to be found in association with other tektites, such as the Moldavites that are found in the Nördlinger Ries crater.

The study of the Moldavite deposits in South Bohemia has helped scientists to understand the formation of tektites and the impact of meteorites on Earth. It has also helped to shed light on the geological history of the region.

**Randomilice**

The Randomilice area is a small area located in the north-east of the Czech Republic. It is a discrete provider field of Moldavite, meaning that it is a small area that produces a relatively high number of Moldavites.

The Moldavites from the Randomilice area are characterized by their high content of silica (83%), which gives them a characteristically softer green color. They also have a low content of bubbles of gas and are well-rounded in shape. The average weight of a Moldavite from the Randomilice area is 9 grams, but the largest stone found in the area weighed 172 grams.

The Moldavites from the Randomilice area are found in Quaternary sediments, which are sediments that are less than 2.6 million years old. These sediments are well-preserved, which means that the Moldavites from the Randomilice area are also well-preserved.

Rare finds of Moldavite have occurred in the northern part of the Randomilice area. These finds suggest that there may be more Moldavites in this area that have not yet been discovered.

The Moldavites from the Randomilice area are prized by collectors for their rarity and beauty. They are also considered to be powerful healing stones.

The Ceske Budejovice and surroundings area and the Cheb area are two of the most important areas for Moldavite production in the Czech Republic.

**The Ceske Budejovice and surroundings**

The Ceske Budejovice and surroundings area is located in the west of South Bohemia. It is the most prolific area for Moldavite production, accounting for about 98% of all Moldavite that has been found. The Moldavites from this area are typically found in fluvial and lacustrine sediments of the Pliocene period. They are thin and almost round in shape, and they have an average weight of 2 to 6 grams. The largest stone found in this area weighed 36 grams.

## The Cheb

The Cheb area is located in the west of Bohemia. It is the second most important area for Moldavite production, accounting for about 2% of all Moldavite that has been found. The Moldavites from this area are typically found in fluvial and lacustrine sediments of the Miocene period. They are also thin and almost round in shape, but they are slightly larger than the Moldavites from the Ceske Budejovice and surroundings area. The largest stone found in this area weighed 25 grams.

The Moldavites from both of these areas are prized by collectors for their rarity and beauty. They are also considered to be powerful healing stones.

## The Trebon

The Trebon area, the Moravia area, and the Horn area are all important areas for Moldavite production.

The Trebon area is located in the east of South Bohemia. It is a smaller area than the Ceske Budejovice and surroundings area, but it has produced a significant number of Moldavites. The Moldavites from this area are typically found in fluvial and lacustrine sediments of the Middle Miocene period. They are angular and fragmented, and they have an average weight of 3 to 20 grams.

## The Moravia

The Moravia area is located to the east of Bohemia. It is the second largest area for Moldavite production, after the Ceske Budejovice and surroundings area. The Moldavites from this area are typically found in fluvial and lacustrine sediments of the Middle Miocene period. They are bottle green in color, and they have an average weight of 10 to 20 grams. The largest stone found in this area weighed 258 grams.

## The Horn

The Horn area is located in the northern part of Austria. It is the smallest of the three areas, but it has produced a few Moldavites. The Moldavites from this area are similar to the Moldavites from the Trebon area, and they have an average weight of 5 to 10 grams.

The Moldavites from all of these areas are prized by collectors for their rarity and beauty. They are also considered to be powerful healing stones.

## The Lusatia

The Lusatia area in Germany is also a small area where Moldavite has been found. The Moldavites from this area are similar to the Moldavites from the Moravia area, and they have an average weight of 5 to 10 grams. The largest stone found in this area weighed 74 grams.

The Moldavites from the Lusatia area are thought to have been transported from the Czech Republic by rivers or glaciers. They are considered to be of the same age as the Moldavites from the Czech Republic, and they have the same composition.

The discovery of Moldavite in the Lusatia area is significant because it suggests that Moldavite may have been more widespread in the past. It is also possible that there are other areas in Germany where Moldavite has not yet been found.

# "Moldavite" Green Stone in The Western Hemisphere

Yes, there have been reports of Moldavite being found in Venezuela. The first samples were obtained in the late 1990s, and the area has been the subject of some exploration and research since then.

The Moldavites from Venezuela are similar to the Moldavites from the Czech Republic in terms of their composition and appearance. They are also thought to have been formed by the impact of a meteorite, but the exact age and origin of the Venezuelan Moldavites is still not fully understood.

The discovery of Moldavite in Venezuela is significant because it suggests that Moldavite may have been more widespread in the past. It is also possible that there are other areas in the Americas where Moldavite has not yet been found.

The study of the Venezuelan Moldavites is ongoing, and scientists are still learning about their properties and origins. However, the discovery of these stones is a significant contribution to the study of tektites and the impact of meteorites on Earth.

# CHAPTER 3

FEATURES OF THE "MOLDAVITE" GREEN STONE

"The gem that fell from the sky"

Referring to the study by the Czech scientist Jan Bouska, who estimated that the total mass of Moldavite that fell to Earth was about 20 tons. This estimate was based on the number of Moldavites that had been found at the time, as well as the average size and weight of the stones.

Bouska's estimate has been revised upwards in recent years, with some scientists now believing that the total mass of Moldavite could be as high as 100 tons. This is because more Moldavites have been found since Bouska's study, and the average size and weight of the stones have also been found to be larger than previously thought.

The quality of Moldavite varies greatly. The most valuable Moldavites are those that are clear and transparent, with a deep green color. These stones are often used in jewelry. Less valuable Moldavites are opaque or have a cloudy appearance. These stones are often used as collectibles.

The color of Moldavite is also variable. The most common color is bottle green, but Moldavite can also be found in yellow, brown, and black. The color of Moldavite is thought to be due to the presence of different minerals in the stone.

The size of Moldavite also varies. The smallest Moldavites are only a few millimeters in size, while the largest Moldavites can weigh several kilograms. The average size of Moldavite is about 4 grams.

The rarity of Moldavite makes it a valuable stone. The most valuable Moldavites are those that are clear, transparent, and have a deep green color. These stones are often used in jewelry and can be very expensive. Less valuable Moldavites are opaque or have a cloudy appearance. These stones are often used as collectibles and are less expensive.

Moldavite classification is based on the quality and appearance of the stone.

- Type A Moldavite is the highest quality Moldavite. It is fully transparent and has no defects. This type of Moldavite is the most valuable and is often used in jewelry.

- Type B Moldavite is not as transparent as Type A Moldavite, but it still has good quality. This type of Moldavite is often used as a collectible.

- Type B Moldavite with sand is the lowest quality Moldavite. It is opaque and has sand or other impurities mixed in with it. This type of Moldavite is not often used in jewelry or as a collectible.

The classification system is not perfect, and there is some overlap between the different types. For example, a Type A Moldavite may have a small bubble or imperfection that would make it a Type AA Moldavite. Ultimately, the classification of Moldavite is a matter of opinion.

The classification system is a useful way to compare different Moldavites and to understand their quality. It can also help you to choose the right Moldavite for your needs. If you are looking for a high-quality Moldavite to use in jewelry, then you should look for a Type A Moldavite. If you are looking for a Moldavite to collect, then you may want to consider a Type B Moldavite.

The Moldavite found in Venezuela is different from the Moldavite found in the Czech Republic in terms of its color, morphology, and surface texture.

It is typically pale green, soft green, or bottle green. It is also typically smooth and free of cracks. This is because the Moldavite in Venezuela has not been eroded or transported as much as the Moldavite in the Czech Republic.

The Moldavite found in the Czech Republic is typically darker green and has a grainier surface. This is because the Moldavite in the Czech Republic has been eroded and transported more than the Moldavite in Venezuela.

The presence of sand attached to some of the Moldavite found in Venezuela is also a sign that it has not been transported as much as the Moldavite found in the Czech Republic. This sand is the same sand that was on the ground when the meteorite impacted, and it was fused to Moldavite during the impact.

The different characteristics of the Moldavite found in Venezuela and the Czech Republic are due to the different geological histories of the two areas. The Moldavite in Venezuela is younger than the Moldavite in the Czech Republic, and it has not been exposed to the same weathering and erosion.

The discovery of Moldavite in Venezuela is a significant contribution to the study of tektites and the impact of meteorites on Earth. It provides evidence that Moldavite can be found in other parts of the world, and it helps us to understand the geological history of Venezuela.

## "Moldavite" Green Stone as Gem

Only a small fraction of Moldavite is suitable for use in jewelry. This is because Moldavite is a very soft stone, and it is easily damaged. Moldavite that is used in jewelry is typically cut into small pieces, or it is used as beads or cabochons.

The most valuable Moldavite is used to make faceted gemstones. Faceted gemstones are cut into specific shapes that enhance their beauty and brilliance. The most common cuts for Moldavite are the emerald cut, the baguette cut, and the round cut.

The emerald cut is a long, rectangular cut that is known for its brilliance. The baguette cut is a long, thin cut that is similar to the emerald cut, but it is narrower. The round cut is a classic cut that is known for its symmetry.

Moldavite that is used in jewelry is typically very expensive. This is because it is a rare and beautiful stone. The price of Moldavite jewelry can range from a few hundred dollars to several thousand dollars.

If you are considering buying Moldavite jewelry, it is important to do your research and buy from a reputable dealer. There are many fake Moldavites on the market, so it is important to make sure that you are buying a genuine stone.

# Green stone "MOLDAVITE" chemical composition

The chemical composition of Moldavite varies depending on the location where it is found. However, there are some common components that are always present in Moldavite, including:

- Silicon dioxide ($SiO_2$): This is the main component of Moldavite, and it makes up about 70% of the stone.

- Aluminum oxide ($Al_2O_3$): This is the second most common component of Moldavite, and it makes up about 10% of the stone.

- Iron oxide ($Fe_2O_3$): This is the third most common component of Moldavite, and it makes up about 3% of the stone.

- Magnesium oxide ($MgO$): This makes up about 2% of Moldavite.

- Calcium oxide ($CaO$): This makes up about 1% of Moldavite.

These are the main components of Moldavite, but there are also other elements present in smaller amounts. These include potassium, sodium, titanium, and zirconium.

The variation in the chemical composition of Moldavite is due to the different materials that were vaporized and melted during the meteorite impact that created the stone. The different proportions of these materials are what give Moldavite its different colors and properties.

The characteristic green color of Moldavite is caused by the presence of iron oxide. The amount of iron oxide present in the stone determines the shade of green. Stones with more iron oxide will be darker green, while stones with less iron oxide will be lighter green.

The presence of other elements, such as potassium and sodium, can also affect the color of Moldavite. Stones with more potassium will be more yellow, while stones with more sodium will be bluer.

The chemical composition of Moldavite is also important because it can be used to identify the stone. Moldavite is a type of tektite, which is natural glass formed by meteorite impacts. The chemical composition of tektites is unique, so it can be used to distinguish them from other types of glass.

**Composition (%)**

**Physical Properties of "Moldavite" Green Stone**

The definition of beauty is subjective and can vary from person to person. However, there are some general qualities that are often considered to be beautiful, such as symmetry, proportion, harmony, and balance.

When it comes to gems, the definition of beauty is even more subjective. Some people may prefer large, clear stones, while others may prefer smaller, more unique stones. There are also different cultures and traditions that have different ideas about what makes a gem beautiful.

However, there are some factors that are generally considered to be important for the beauty of a gem. These include:

- Color: The color of a gem is one of the most important factors that affects its beauty. Different colors evoke different emotions and can be associated with different meanings. For example, red is often associated with passion, while blue is associated with peace.

- Clarity: The clarity of a gem refers to how free it is from flaws. A gem with high clarity will be more transparent and will have a more brilliant appearance.

- Cut: The cut of a gem refers to the way it has been shaped. A well-cut gem will reflect light in a way that enhances its beauty.

- Carat weight: The carat weight of a gem refers to its weight in carats. A carat is equal to 200 milligrams. Larger gems are often more valuable, but this is not always the case.

- Rarity: The rarity of a gem also affects its value. Gems that are rare are often more valuable, even if they are not as large or clear as other gems.

Ultimately, the beauty of a gem is a matter of personal opinion. However, the factors listed above are some of the most important considerations for those who are looking for a beautiful gem.

The four C's are the most important factors that affect the value of a gem. They are:

**Color:** The color of a gem is one of the most important factors that affects its value. Different colors evoke different emotions and can be associated with different meanings. For example, red is often associated with passion, while blue is associated with peace.

**Clarity:** The clarity of a gem refers to how free it is from flaws. A gem with high clarity will be more transparent and will have a more brilliant appearance.

**Cut:** The cut of a gem refers to the way it has been shaped. A well-cut gem will reflect light in a way that enhances its beauty.

**Carat weight:** The carat weight of a gem refers to its weight in carats. A carat is equal to 200 milligrams. Larger gems are often more valuable, but this is not always the case.

The four C's are also important for Moldavite. Moldavite is a type of tektite, which is natural glass formed by meteorite impacts. Moldavite is typically green in color, but it can also be found in other colors, such as yellow, brown, and black. The clarity of Moldavite can vary, but the most valuable Moldavite is clear and free of flaws. The cut of Moldavite can also affect its value. A well-cut Moldavite will reflect light in a way that enhances its beauty.

The rarity of Moldavite also affects its value. Moldavite is a rare stone, and it is only found in a few places in the world. This makes it a valuable and sought-after stone.

The four C's are a good starting point for understanding the value of a gem. However, there are other factors that can also affect the value of a gem, such as its history and provenance.

**The hardness**

The hardness of a gem is a measure of its ability to resist scratching. The Mohs scale is a scale of mineral hardness that is used to measure the relative hardness of different materials. The Mohs scale is numbered from 1 to 10, with 1 being the softest and 10 being the hardest.

Diamond is the hardest natural substance on Earth, with a Mohs hardness of 10. The next hardest natural substance is corundum, which has a Mohs hardness of 9. Other hard natural substances include topaz (8), garnet (7.5), and apatite (5).

Moldavite has a Mohs hardness of 6.5 to 7, which makes it a relatively hard stone. It is harder than most other gems, but it is not as hard as diamond or corundum.

The resistance of a gem is a measure of its ability to resist wear and tear. The resistance of a gem is affected by its hardness, as well as its chemical composition and structure.

Diamond is the most resistant gem, followed by corundum. Other resistant gems include topaz, garnet, and apatite.

Moldavite has an intermediate resistance. It is more resistant than most other gems, but it is not as resistant as diamond or corundum.

The hardness and resistance of a gem are important factors to consider when choosing a gem for jewelry or other applications. Hard gems are less likely to be scratched or damaged, while resistant gems are less likely to wear out or break.

## The stability

The stability of a gem is a measure of its resistance to changes in its physical and chemical properties. The stability of a gem is affected by its chemical composition and structure.

Moldavite is a very stable gem. It is not affected by heat, ultraviolet rays, or chemicals. It is also not affected by changes in temperature or humidity.

The stability of Moldavite is one of the reasons why it is so valuable. It is a gem that can be worn and enjoyed for many years without fear of damage.

Here are some of the factors that can affect the stability of a gem:

**Chemical composition:** The chemical composition of a gem determines its physical and chemical properties. Gems with a high concentration of silica are generally more stable than gems with a low concentration of silica.

**Crystal structure:** The crystal structure of a gem also affects its stability. Gems with a regular crystal structure are generally more stable than gems with an irregular crystal structure.

**Treatments:** Some gems are treated to improve their appearance or durability. These treatments can affect the stability of the gem.

It is important to be aware of the factors that can affect the stability of a gem when choosing a gem for jewelry or other applications. Stable gems are less likely to change color, break, or lose their luster over time.

## Gravity

The specific gravity of a gem is a measure of its density. The specific gravity is the ratio of the weight of a gem to the weight of an equal volume of water.

The specific gravity of Moldavite is 2.35 to 2.40, which is slightly higher than the specific gravity of water (1.0). This means that Moldavite is about 2.4 times heavier than water.

The specific gravity of a gem is affected by its chemical composition and crystal structure. Gems with a high concentration of heavier elements, such as iron and nickel, will have a higher specific gravity than gems with a lower concentration of these elements.

The specific gravity of a gem is a useful property for identification purposes. It can be used to distinguish between different types of gems and to determine if a gem is genuine or synthetic.

Here are some of the factors that can affect the specific gravity of a gem:

- Chemical composition: The chemical composition of a gem determines its density. Gems with a high concentration of heavier elements, such as iron and nickel, will have a higher specific gravity than gems with a lower concentration of these elements.

- Crystal structure: The crystal structure of a gem also affects its density. Gems with a regular crystal structure will have a higher specific gravity than gems with an irregular crystal structure.

- Temperature: The temperature of a gem can affect its specific gravity. Gems will become less dense as they are heated up.

- Pressure: The pressure of a gem can affect its specific gravity. Gems will become denser as they are subjected to pressure.

It is important to be aware of the factors that can affect the specific gravity of a gem when using it for identification purposes.

## THE GREEN STONE "MOLDAVITE" (OPTICAL PROPERTIES)

Optical properties are those that are related to the behavior of light, on, or in, a gemstone. Some of these can be seen, and even quantified, with the naked eye alone. Three such characteristics are: luster, transparency, and color.

Luster is the way light reflects off the surface of a gemstone. It is often described as being metallic, vitreous, or pearly.

Transparency refers to how much light can pass through a gemstone. Transparent gemstones allow all of the light to pass through, translucent gemstones allow some of the light to pass through, and opaque gemstones do not allow any light to pass through.

Color is the most obvious optical property of a gemstone. It is caused by the absorption of certain wavelengths of light by the gemstone.

Other optical properties of gemstones that require laboratory instruments to be measured include:

The refractive index is the measure of how much light bends when it passes through a gemstone.

Birefringence is the measure of how much light is split into two rays when it passes through a gemstone.

Pleochroism is the ability of a gemstone to show different colors when viewed from different angles.

Dispersion is the ability of a gemstone to split white light into its component colors.

Reaction to ultraviolet rays is the way a gemstone reacts to ultraviolet light. Some gemstones will fluoresce, or glow, when exposed to ultraviolet light. Others will phosphoresce, or glow, for a short period of time after being exposed to ultraviolet light.

These optical properties are important for gem identification and grading. They can also be used to create different effects in jewelry, such as cat's eye or starburst.

The gloss of Moldavite is one of the factors that determines its value. The highest quality Moldavite is known for its glassy, almost oily luster. This is due to the high concentration of silica in Moldavite, which gives it a smooth and polished surface.

Lower quality Moldavite may have a more matte or dull luster. This is due to the presence of inclusions or impurities in the stone. Inclusions are small particles of other minerals that are trapped within Moldavite during its formation. Impurities are chemical elements that are present in the stone but are not part of its normal chemical composition.

**The Gloss**

The gloss of Moldavite is also affected by its cutting. Well-cut Moldavite will have a more uniform luster than poorly cut Moldavite. This is because the cutting process removes any rough or uneven surfaces on the stone, which can reflect light unevenly.

If you are looking for a piece of Moldavite with a high gloss, you should look for a stone that is classified as "Gem" or "AAA" quality. These stones will have a smooth, polished surface that reflects light beautifully.

Here are some tips for evaluating the gloss of Moldavite:

Hold the stone in your hand and rotate it so that you can see it from different angles.

Look for a stone that has a smooth, uniform surface.

Avoid stones that have any rough or uneven surfaces.

If possible, compare the stone to other pieces of Moldavite to see how its gloss compares.

With a little practice, you will be able to quickly and easily evaluate the gloss of Moldavite and choose a stone that is right for you.

**The transparency**

The transparency of a gemstone is one of the most important factors that determines its value. It is defined as the ability of light to pass through the stone without being scattered or absorbed.

Transparent gemstones allow all of the light to pass through them, while translucent gemstones allow some of the light to pass through. Opaque gemstones do not allow any light to pass through them.

The transparency of Moldavite can range from semi-translucent to transparent. The most valuable Moldavite is completely transparent, allowing light to pass through it without any obstruction. This type of Moldavite is rare and highly sought-after.

The transparency of Moldavite is affected by a number of factors, including its thickness, the presence of inclusions, and its chemical composition. Thicker Moldavite is less transparent than thinner Moldavite. Moldavite that contains inclusions, such as gas bubbles or other minerals, is also less transparent. Moldavite with a high concentration of iron is also less transparent.

If you are looking for a piece of Moldavite, you should look for a stone that is as transparent as possible. This will give you the best possible view of the stone's color and internal characteristics.

Here are some tips for evaluating the transparency of Moldavite:

- Hold the stone up to a light source and look for any obstructions to the light.

- If you can see through the stone clearly, it is transparent.

- If you can see any inclusions or bubbles, the stone is translucent.

- If you cannot see through the stone at all, it is opaque.

With a little practice, you will be able to quickly and easily evaluate the transparency of Moldavite and choose a stone that is right for you.

**The refractive**

The refractive index of a gemstone is a measure of how much light bends when it passes through the stone. It is calculated by dividing the speed of light in a vacuum by the speed of light in the stone.

The refractive index of Moldavite ranges from 1.48 to 1.52. This means that light travels about 1.48 to 1.52 times slower in Moldavite than it does in a vacuum.

The refractive index of a gemstone is affected by its chemical composition and density. Moldavite is a type of tektite, which is a natural glass formed from molten rock that was ejected from the Earth's surface during a meteorite impact. The high silica content of Moldavite gives it a high refractive index.

The refractive index of a gemstone can be used to identify the stone and to determine its quality. Gemstones with a higher refractive index are generally more valuable than those with a lower refractive index.

Here are some other factors that affect the refractive index of a gemstone:

- Temperature: The refractive index of a gemstone decreases with increasing temperature.

- Pressure: The refractive index of a gemstone increases with increasing pressure.

- Composition: The refractive index of a gemstone is affected by its chemical composition. For example, gemstones with a higher concentration of iron have a higher refractive index.

- Crystal structure: The refractive index of a gemstone is also affected by its crystal structure. For example, gemstones with a cubic crystal structure have a higher refractive index than those with a hexagonal crystal structure.

**Color**

The color of Moldavite is caused by the presence of iron in the stone. Iron atoms can absorb certain wavelengths of light, and the remaining wavelengths are reflected back to our eyes. This is what gives Moldavite its characteristic green color.

The exact shade of green in Moldavite can vary depending on the amount and type of iron present in the stone. Moldavite can range in color from light green to dark green, and some stones may even have a brown tint.

The most valuable Moldavite is typically the darkest green, as this indicates that it contains the most iron. However, some people prefer lighter shades of green, as they believe that these stones are gentler and calming.

The color of Moldavite is also affected by its cutting. Well-cut Moldavite will show off its natural beauty to the best advantage. However, even poorly cut Moldavite can still be a beautiful and valuable stone.

If you are looking for a piece of Moldavite, you should consider the color that you prefer. There is no right or wrong answer, as it is a matter of personal taste. However, you should also consider the quality of the stone and its cutting when making your decision.

**Characteristics of the samples**

the characteristics of Moldavites found in the Cheb basin in Czech Republic and in Venezuela.

The Moldavites found in the Cheb basin are similar to those found in the Ceske Budejovice-Trebon region in South Bohemia. They are typically bottle green in color, with a high content of bubbles and grains. They are also somewhat softer to the touch than Moldavites from other regions.

The Moldavites found in Venezuela are also bottle green in color, but they are opaquer than those found in the Czech Republic. They are also smaller and less common.

Here is a table summarizing the characteristics of Moldavites found in the Cheb basin and in Venezuela:

| Characteristic | Cheb basin | Venezuela |
| --- | --- | --- |
| Color | Bottle green | Bottle green |
| Opacity | Transparent | Opaque |
| Size | Larger | Smaller |
| Commonality | More common | Less common |
| Softness | Softer | Hard |
| Content of bubbles and grains | High | Low |

## Overview

The evidence that supports the claim that Moldavites are meteorites from outer space.

The evidence for this claim comes from a variety of sources, including:

- Chemical analysis: Moldavites have a unique chemical composition that is similar to other tektites, which are natural glasses formed from meteorite impacts.

- Physical properties: Moldavites have a high melting point and a low density, which are also characteristic of tektites.

- Petrographic analysis: Moldavites have a glassy texture with small bubbles and inclusions, which are consistent with their formation from a molten material.

- Stratigraphic distribution: Moldavites are found in a specific layer of sedimentary rock, which suggests that they were deposited at the same time as the impact that formed the rock.

- Age dating: Moldavites have been dated to be around 14.7 million years old, which is consistent with the age of the impact that formed the Bohemian Massif.

The evidence for the extraterrestrial origin of Moldavites is strong and convincing. However, there is still some debate about the exact nature of the impact that formed them. Some scientists believe that they were formed from the impact of a comet, while others believe that they were formed from the impact of an asteroid.

The discovery of Moldavites in Venezuela is further evidence of their extraterrestrial origin. The distance between Venezuela and the Bohemian Massif is about 16 million light years, which is a very long way for a meteorite to travel. This suggests that Moldavites were formed by a very large impact event, which would have released a large amount of energy.

The discovery of Moldavites in Venezuela is also significant because it suggests that there may be other meteorites from this impact event that have yet to be found. This could lead to new discoveries about the history of our solar system.

# CHAPTER 4



"The gem that fell from the sky"

## Nicholas and Helena

Nicholas and Helena Roerich were a remarkable couple who dedicated their lives to promoting peace and understanding. They were both highly accomplished individuals, and their work together had a profound impact on the world.

Nicholas Roerich was a Russian painter, writer, and philosopher. He was known for his beautiful and spiritual paintings, which often depicted the Himalayas and other sacred landscapes. He was also a tireless advocate for peace, and he founded the Banner of Peace movement, which promotes understanding and cooperation between cultures.

Helena Roerich was a Russian writer and mystic. She was the author of several books on spiritual topics, including the popular book Agni Yoga. She was also a gifted artist, and her paintings often reflected her spiritual insights.

The Roerichs traveled extensively throughout their lives, and they spent many years in India and Central Asia. They were deeply influenced by the cultures they encountered, and they incorporated many of these influences into their work.

The Roerichs' work continues to inspire people around the world. They are remembered as two of the most important figures in the history of peace and spirituality.

**Nicolay Roerich**

The connection between Nicholas Roerich and the Chintamani stone.

The Chintamani stone is a mythical gem that is said to have many magical properties, including the ability to grant wishes and bring peace and prosperity. It is often associated with the lost Kingdom of Shambhala, which is said to be located in the Himalayas.

Nicholas Roerich was a Russian painter, writer, and philosopher who was interested in the mystical and spiritual aspects of the world. He was also a strong advocate for peace and understanding. Some people believe that Roerich was in possession of a Chintamani stone, and that he used it to help him achieve his goals.

There is no evidence to support the claim that Roerich was in possession of a Chintamani stone. However, the fact that he was interested in the stone and its symbolism suggests that he may have believed in its power.

The Chintamani stone is a fascinating and mysterious object. Its origins and powers are unknown, but it continues to fascinate people today. Whether or not Nicholas Roerich was in possession of a Chintamani stone, he was a remarkable individual who made a significant contribution to the world.

**Helena Roerich**

The legend of the stone that Helena Roerich wrote about in her book At the Crossroads of the Orient.

The legend tells the story of a green stone that was brought to Earth by emissaries from a planet orbiting the star Sirius. The stone was given to the King of Shambhala, who used it to bring peace and prosperity to his kingdom. The stone was said to have many magical properties, including the ability to grant wishes and heal the sick.

" We reproduce all of that section of the book, because the end some things of great interest to us.

## "AT THE CROSSROADS OF THE EAST"

## "THE LEGEND OF THE STONE"

I come across the desert - I will bring the calyx covered with shield. Inside is a treasure - the gift of Orion. Oh you, bearer of the flame, recalls Lob-Nor and spread your camp. Kuku-Nor - Steed hurries.

And in the Temple of Judea, the bearer of the flame does not take. And Passedvan just saved her; with it, the stone left behind the ruins of China. You do not strive for stone. She will come one if you know how to expect it.

***

More, betrayal, the servants of the temple usurped the stone from the hands of the sovereign of the India to glorify a foreign land. That pride that mountain hide the stone for a while. The city of the stone to be glorified. But the trail of treasure has already been ordered. It is time that the stone returns home.

When on the chalice flame thread in a ring, my time is coming.

***

On the island of Lanka lies the stone hidden by the perfidy of Ravana. The stone will depart overseas. In its wake, as the tail of the Comet, happiness is still in flames; but not for much longer.

That the hundreds of steps of China welcome to the bearer of the flame. More Passedvan takes the stone. And Sands transmit fire to the fearless rider, Grayling. One that is big is approaching the amber wall and covered the field with their banners. "That stone rests in the Temple until my return." More life led to the miracle to the grandson. The stone road turned towards the West.

***

The underground religious parents are assembled to analyze the nature of the stone. "Would the clouds, when stone turns dark, accumulate? When the stone feels heavy, there is bloodshed. When a star is shining on the stone, success comes. When the stone creaks, the enemy approaches. When the stone comes from a dream on fire, the world is in turmoil. When the stone is still, walk with courage. Most don't pour wine over the stone! Burns on her only Cedar Balsam. It takes the stone in a chest of ivory.

As well as one must get used to the cold and heat, so must one get accustomed to the glow of the stone. Each of the carriers of the stone should dwell with her quietly for a while. Its ray intoxication is invisible, but its internal heat is more powerful than radium. Myrrh flows without being seen more stone rests visible on the network in his homeland.

***

In the middle of the breath of the steppe and the crystalline resonance of the mountains, the spirit of the stone points the way from the banner. The miracle of the rays of Orion is leading persons. The master leads the horses to the high Yutzakis and Karakorum Nor. The demonstration is expected in Uyûb-Nor.

***

The priestly knowledge of all-time prepares men for the worthy reception of the treasure. Long ago laws of wisdom revealed the day when a double eclipse and the submersion of the sanctities will mark the new advent of stone. We hope our destiny in prayer!

Oh, stone, begins from the sea. That bird will bring new - stone ear is coming.

***

In the darkness of the night mysteriously dressed, the Messenger silently approaches to see how to expect them. At the turn of a corner lies waiting for a tame beast, sniffing, snooping with claws; He has been sent by the enemy. Who stirred behind the window? What flies are swarming the place? From where does the whirlwind come? But I walk firm and insurance: I am holding the stone.

I'm learning the prayer: do not forsake me, my Lord! I have met all the force. Do not forsake me I'm already going towards you!

***

The burning stone lies in Mount Ararat. A gentleman of Novgorod was killed on the stone due to skepticism. The great freedom of Novgorod proved the possession of the treasure more heresy turned the fulfillment of the miracle.

The best relic of the power of the stone is symbolized by the snake - symbol of a wise possession stone.

The follower of the night sought to regain possession of the stone. More treasure was always the light signal. The crafty and devious sovereigns do not possess the stone much time without realizing that the effort by right can govern the stone fire.

***

Uroil Zena, the spirit of the air, took the stone to King Solomon. The spirit is proclaimed a receptive ear: "by the will of the Lord of powers I you charge the Treasury of the Lord's powers. I commend the treasure of the world."

So be,' said the King and the stone was carried to the temple.

But the thought of carrying part of the treasure in his person possessed it. Then the King summoned Ephraim, the Goldsmith of the tribe of Judah; He ordered that it cut a part of the stone with pure silver solugap ring and recorded on the stone Goblet of wisdom lit a flame. The King never thought of starting with the treasure. But the spirit said, "it was not wise that you rape the Supreme substance. For the sons of men will be painfully difficult to own stone. And only those who are with you may direct the stone toward righteousness. By a constellation I will appoint the road of stone."

**Split the Messenger where Khan Tamerlane.**

Worried lies the stone at Otakuye. An escort with three banners must be dispatched. The men travel on camels. A tower of sand darkens the Sun. Items hidden to travelers. They are traveling tirelessly. And the kayuks return the horses to the home. Who will protect the stone at night? The desert hides strangers and with them the stone was to the South. It reflects, Khan, how to reach the stone correctly. Came the pain and disease; even the horse lost its way. The manifested spirit approached noble riders: "do not seek". The time itself will reveal them their way."

Each Ulus sings its own song about the stone.

***

Father Sulpicius had a vision: a white column of clouds appeared before him. She came with a voice: "keep the stone altar brought from Rothenburg. On the altar there are four squares and in each sign M. The demonstration will be revealed when I pronounced the four eastward March! Nothing should diminish the commandment. Surrender before the intended time. I will gather my star warriors. Anyone who is ordered to recognize the appointed time, you will have to gather. This I bear witness it at this time, stone is set up as a human heart within this a glowing Crystal will be saved."

With these words the column spread in blue Sparks, making the very shaky father Sulpicius. This is the biggest wonder that the stone from the East has the oblong shape of fruit flat or heart. On the altar were found the letters spoken previously. Its meaning is unknown.

***

The sovereign Kurnovoo, loaded with gold, received the black stone sent from Tazlavoo containing the Crystal of life, and on the gold sovereign had put the stone.

***

Tristan's book, called Mon: "when the son of the Sun descended on Earth to teach humanity, fell from the sky a shield carrying the power to the world. In the center of the shield between the three different brands were signs of silver predicting events under the rays of the Sun. The sudden darkening of the Sun made despair the son of the Sun and he dropped the shield and was destroyed. Bad omen was the constellation. More power was the central fragment - there landed the ray of the Sun.

"It is said that King Solomon cut the central portion of the stone for your ring. The legend of our priests also shattered the sun shield. The most deplorable error is the denied stone.

"Truly, I myself saw this fragment of the world - I remember your way - as long as my little finger - a grayish glow as a dried fruit." Even I remember the signs but could not understand them.

"Certainly I myself saw the stone and I will find it. It is said that the stone comes from itself; It cannot be taken. If so, I'm going to wait for her. Because of it I will go to the desert, until the end of my days."

"Mon, remember, you decided to wait for it!

***

When the stone was lost to the sovereign of India, his wife said, "We will find it again. The valiant demanded an arc; he was going to take down the bird"

***

When the Emperor of China had the treasure of the Sun, he erected a turquoise Temple azure-blue like the sky. When the little Prince and his girlfriend are loomed behind the door, the Emperor said. "Fox is leading them. You feel the joy of the world."

***

Remember the Lombard Iron Crown; that is also a trace of stone. Not long ago the stone rested near the mountain of dignity. Many are the messengers of the East. The camels bring the stone to Tibet. They carry it across the desert and with it a new power.

And its last flight to the West illuminated an unknown Kingdom of a failed union of Western Nations. In each beam from the East, they already seek the stone.

The time will come; dates will be met. Designated is the way that is prescribed when the stone comes from the West.

We say what to expect and understand the stone way. We say understand predestined carriers stone who are directed toward home. The boat is ready.

***

The new country will come out to find the seven stars under the sign of the three stars that sent the stone to the world. The treasure is prepared, and the enemy will not take the shield covered with gold.

Wait for the stone!

This book was written in 1930 and in Russian language and later translated into other languages.

Once consumed the facts, it is relatively easy to correlate them, but if someone provided them to us and presented them in one way or another. The following sentence predicted that the stone will be watching. The paragraph is:

"In its last flight to the West illuminated an unknown Kingdom of a failed union of Western Nations. These, now, seek the stone in every ray of the East.

The time will come; dates will be met. The predestined path has been chosen when the stone comes itself to the West."

Undoubtedly, in addition, it indicates that the stone will be shown in the West; he mentions a country unknown at that time and a failed union of Nations.

I don't know why this reminds me unfortunately the dream of Bolivar to try to form the great Colombia and also the latest misadventure of a low-frequency energy dictator who is currently in Venezuela and who fortunately has failed in his attempt of a union of Nations.

He also mentions that the arrival of the stone will occur in time and predestined dates, which already have been met, if the stone has come, we are at that time.

For some of us there is no doubt of the country which is mentioning. But if this were little, we are going to continue with the text of the book:

"We look forward to and affirm to know the path of the stone. We say: it's known who is predestined as carriers of the stone, who are directed toward home. The boat is ready."

"The stone will be meeting in the new country from the seven stars under the sign of the three stars that sent the stone to the world. The treasure is prepared, and the enemy will not take the shield covered with gold."

We must remember that throughout the book mentioned, the stone is synonymous with a coat of arms, for example:

"When the son of the Sun descended on Earth to teach humanity, fell from the sky a shield carrying power to the world. In the center of the shield between the three different brands were signs of silver predicting events under the rays of the Sun. The sudden darkening of the Sun made despair to the son of the Sun despair. He dropped the shield, and this is smashing. The bad omen was the constellation. More power was the central fragment - there landed the ray of the Sun.

"It is said that King Solomon cut the central portion of the stone for his ring. The legend of our priests also shattered sun shield. "The most deplorable error is the denied stone."

Because of this, we can consider that when it comes to shield, is the protection provided by the stone.

Returning to the country of the seven stars; someone still is left any doubt which country is concerned? "What is the country that had seven stars on its flag?"

"Is there any doubt that the mentioned country where "Moldavite" green stone would be found is Venezuela?" Venezuela had seven stars in its flag in the 2oth century.

"What is the sign of the three stars that sent the stone to the world?"

Where does the green stone (Moldavite) comes?. Is it from "The constellation of Canis Maioris or the constellation of Orion", represented by the triple star of Sirius or the three stars of the belt of Orion?

# REFERENCES

## Maitreya

The word Maitreya is derived from the Sanskrit term maitrī, which means a compassionate and friendly bond. The prophecy of Maitreya is found in all Buddhist traditions. According to the Mahayana Buddhism's Maitreya vyakarana, Maitreya will become the Buddha in India, although the current continents will be different. He will be born into a world that is spiritually advanced, and at that time, people's basic needs will already be met, and there will be a state of complete world peace. However, the people of that era will not remember the Dharma, and Maitreya will appear to remind them of its importance and show it to them again with clarity. All the stories and various comments about Maitreya follow this scenario.

## LOB-Nor

The Tarim River empties into the Lake system, which is the only remaining part of the historic Lake Tarim. This lake once covered over ten thousand square kilometers of the Tarim River basin. Lop Nor is one of the largest endorheic watersheds in the world. The Kingdom of Lulan, an ancient civilization on the Silk Road, flourished on the northwestern shore of the historic Lake, thanks to the ancient resources of water from the Tarim River and Lop Nor. However, that culture is now buried in the sands of the Lop desert. Lulan became the Kingdom of Shanshan, a satellite state of the Chinese Empire, from 55 BC onwards. The end of the Lake's existence brought an end of life and flourishing culture. Buried settlements and Tarim mummies have been discovered along the ancient shores of the Lake. European explorers such as Marco Polo, Baron von Richthofen, Nikolai Przhevalsky, and Sven Hedin visited the Lop Nor area during the 19th and 20th centuries.

## Kuku-Nor

It is a large lake in Mongolia, which has said in the past he was in Tibet, in the place where their capital Lassa is located underground.

## Rāvana

In Hindu mythology, Rāvana was the King of the demons rakshasas. Her abduction of Sītā (the wife of the god

Krishna) and his death in the hands of this are the main facts of the ancient epic text Ramayana.

**Karakoram**

The Karakoram mountain range is situated in the Gilgit-Baltistan region and is one of the largest mountain ranges in Asia, along with the Himalayas. It spans about 500 km across the India-China border in Pakistan and is known for having the highest concentration of glaciers outside of the polar regions.

**Shambhala**

There are generally two main versions regarding the concept of a physical place. One version suggests that it corresponds to a spiritual dimension that only those with a pure heart can access. The other version considers it to be a physical place, more or less inaccessible, possessing advanced technology. This place is believed to be a source of wisdom and youth, with a warm and fertile microclimate, and surrounded by snow-capped mountains in perfect peace and harmony with nature. In India, it is considered a place lost in the Himalayas, while among the Chinese it is believed to be located somewhere in the Kun Lun Mountains. Madame Blavatsky, the founder of the Theosophical Society, wrote about this place, stating that it was the residence of a great fraternity of spiritual masters who guide and protect humanity, sometimes indirectly and clandestinely.

There are four places around the world that are said to have spiritual significance: Mongolia, Iguazu Falls (Brazil-Argentina), the Mato Grosso region in Brazil, and the Himalayas (specifically, Tibet). In Tibet, the legend of Shambhala is associated with Buddhism. It is believed to be a place of wisdom, peace and prosperity, with kind rulers and spiritually evolved citizens. According to the legend, Shakyamuni Buddha transmitted his teachings to the first King of Shambhala, and the citizens began to practice meditation and follow the Buddhist path. As a result, the population of Shambhala became highly evolved beings. However, it is unclear whether Shambhala is a physical place or if it only exists as symbolic signs. In the 19th century, the master of the Mipham wrote about Shambhala in his "great commentary on the Kalachakra". He described it as being north of the river Sita and divided by 8 chains of mountains. The Kalapa Palace of its rulers would be built on the Summit of a circular mountain called Kailasa, in the center of the country. Other versions of the legend suggest that all the inhabitants of Shambhala reached enlightenment, and at that moment, the whole Kingdom disappeared from the physical plane to exist in a spiritual dimension. The rulers of Shambhala also ensure that the land is well taken care of, and one day they will return to save humanity from possible destruction.

There is a belief in the West that a mythical place exists, where the last of a just and happy society desires to live. Although they may be legends, they are said to have originated from one of the historic Eastern Kingdoms from a very remote time. Helena Roerich, the wife of Nicholas Roerich, believed that her husband possessed a stone that symbolized hope and inspiration. She thought it could help bring about a better world. The legend of this stone is a mysterious and fascinating story. It is unclear whether Nicholas Roerich was actually in possession of the magical stone, but the tale continues to inspire people today.

The legend of the stone is a mysterious story, inspiring many today. It is unclear if Nicholas Roerich possessed a magical stone.

# CHAPTER 5

LEGENDS OF THE EAST

STORIES, MYTHS, LEGENDS, AND MORE

"The gem that fell from the sky"

We stand at a crossroads of history, having entered the Age of Aquarius and closed the Era of Pisces. It is time to wake up and understand our mission on Earth. As human beings, we must now recognize our full potential. The work of humanity during the Piscean Age has begun to bear fruit, and we are ready to leap forward. During this era, we can expect significant changes that will affect all of humanity.

In the latter part of the last millennium, during the Age of Darkness, our knowledge and spiritual development were limited. Fortunately, this is no longer the case. We are now making progress and living in a much higher vibration. Self-knowledge, education, and the thirst for discovery have slowly begun to correct the errors caused by illiteracy and fear in the past. Collectively, we are better able than ever to accept, understand, and manage the powers we have, such as those of Moldavite crystals, which emit very high frequencies.

The universe has been waiting patiently for us to develop our capacity for understanding and compressing the powers we have. The time has come. The legends and recent events tell us this is true, and we must act.

We will now discuss some of the most popular legends associated with Moldavite. Most of the best-known legends come from Asia, Africa, and Europe, and we will call these the "Legends of the East." We will discuss these legends in this chapter. Other legends, much less known and popular, come from the Americas, and we will call these the "Legends of the West." We will discuss these legends in the next chapter.

**The origin of the stone**

The history of the green stone "Moldavite" dates back to ancient times, when it first arrived on Earth. There are numerous legends and hypotheses surrounding its origin, but none of them have scientific evidence to support them. However, the explanations given in previous chapters, along with photographs and narrations about the stone, confirm that it is of meteoric origin. It is believed that the stone fell to Earth during a cosmic meteor shower around 16 million years ago. While some ancient Asian chronicles mention that the stone comes from the Orion system, this statement has yet to be confirmed.

I have personally experienced the unique vibrations of two Moldavite stones that I always carry in my pockets. One is a beautiful green color, while the other is a yellowish-green or yellowish-brown shade. When I showed the green stone to a friend's sister during a Christmas gathering, she recognized it as belonging to a friend of hers. This was surprising, as the stone is not easy to obtain. When I contacted this person, he confirmed that he had received the stone from his older brothers, who had told him it was a special and powerful stone. He declined to meet with me at that time but suggested that we may meet in the future.

In conclusion, the only confirmed fact about Moldavite is that it comes from outer space. While there are many legends and stories surrounding its origin, there is no scientific evidence to support them.

**Chronicles of the oldest in Asia**

There are ancient Chronicles of Asia that suggest a stone came from the stars and was delivered by a Messenger angel to Tazlavoo, Emperor of Atlantis. According to legend, the stone was also sent to King Solomon in Israel from Tibet using a mystical flying machine called Vimana. The Vimana is described in ancient Indian literature and was said to be able to fly in the Earth's atmosphere, travel underwater, and even in space. The Vedas describe Vimanas of various sizes and shapes, including a car or chariot of the gods that could move by itself and carry its occupant through the air. The stone mentioned in the texts is believed to be a "Moldavite" with magical properties that fell to Earth in the form of a meteorite approximately 15 million years ago.

In ancient Hindu literature, such as the Ramayana, there are references to flying cars and otherworldly elements that were used during the wars between the Kings of high Asian antiquity. These flying vehicles were able to transport individuals to the heavens and to distant worlds, and then bring them back to Earth. In one instance, a character named Vibhishana offers to take another character to their hometown using a chariot called Pushpaka, which is said to be incomparably beautiful and run by itself. The chariot is described as resembling the sun and is able to transport individuals without concern. Vibhishana is accompanied by his brother and illustrious Videhana, while Raghuaida is already mounted on the chariot. Sugriva and his generals are also invited to ride along with VIBHISHANA, the monarch of the Rakshsas.

The Ramayana, an ancient Hindu literature, mentions flying cars and otherworldly elements that were used during the wars between the Kings of high Asian antiquity. These vehicles were able to transport individuals to the heavens and to distant worlds, and then bring them back to Earth. There is a reference to a chariot named Pushpaka that is described as incomparably beautiful and run by itself, resembling the sun. Vibhishana and Sugriva, along with the Kings of the apes and their ministers, assembled on the large chariot Pushpaka, and it was raised to the bosom of heaven. The vehicle was flying like a big cloud being pushed by wind. They saw the Palace of RAGHU's mother and AYODHYA before them. The people in the city saw them arrive like a second Sun and welcomed them with powerful shouts of joy. BHARATA, from sadness to joy, approached with folded hands and honored the branch. It is said that the stone mentioned in the legend had magical properties and is considered to be green stone crystals known as "Moldavite". The great sacred Black Stone within the Kabah in Mecca, which all Muslims revere, is also considered a large fragment of the meteorite, and it could well be the same stone green (Moldavite).

## Stone Chintamani (Chimtamani Stone)

The Chintamani Stone is also known as the "treasure of the world." It appeared on Earth thousands of light years before the green stone Moldavite and was carried by Russian Mystic Nicholas Roerich to meet with its stone mother in the heart of the far East. The stone was part of a massive jewel that resided in Shambhala, the land of the immortals. Allegedly of extraterrestrial origin, emissaries from a planet orbiting the Syrian star brought the Chintamani Stone to Earth and handed it over to the King of Shambhala, also known as the "King of the world." This monarch is only known by a handful of occultists in the West, but many Mystics in the East are aware of his identity.

In legends of the Holy Grail, the Chintamani Stone is often referred to as the "Stone of heaven," and is synonymous with the Holy Grail. Wolfram von Eschenbach's interpretation of the Grail, known as Parzival, is considered by many scholars to be the most complete and authoritative of Grail legends.

The Chintamani Stone is an intriguing and mysterious artifact that has captured the imagination of many scholars and mystics. Its origins are shrouded in myth and legend, with some claiming that it came from the stars themselves. The stone is said to possess incredible power, including the ability to make a human being immortal. It is also believed to be related to the Holy Grail, and many have speculated that it could be the original source of the philosopher's stone. Despite its many mysteries, the Chintamani Stone remains a fascinating object of study and research.

The Chintamani Stone is a fascinating artifact with a rich history and many legends surrounding it. Some believe it was brought to Earth by Syrian missionaries with the noble aim of developing a civilization based on mutual support, love, and equality among beings. It is said to possess incredible power, including the ability to make a human being immortal, and is believed to be related to the Holy Grail and the philosopher's stone. Throughout history, the stone has been in the possession of planetary rulers and organizations with the power to influence the world on a large scale. It was even given to the founders of the League of Nations, who aimed to create a civilization free of hatred and war. The Chintamani Stone remains an object of study and research, with its mysteries continuing to capture the imagination of scholars and mystics.

Many historians have debated whether Mr. Roerich was able to complete his journey to Shambhala and find the Chintamani Stone. Although technically he failed to reach Shambhala, he did visit a Tibetan site closely linked to it, the Tashilumpo monastery in Shigatse. Legends say that this monastery has tunnels connecting it to Shambhala, and high priests have traveled through these tunnels physically over hundreds of light years. The Panchen Lama, one of the highest lamas of Tibet, is also closely linked to Shigatze and Shambhala through the Kalachakra Tantra. Madame Blavatsky and her student Alice Bailey also visited Shigatse to study with the great white brotherhood and acquire information for their books on esoteric history. Some tribes in Africa claim to have been visited by Syrian missionaries in ancient times and were given knowledge about the grouping of three stars in the Sirius system and the moons surrounding certain planets in our solar system. The Chintamani Stone is said to possess the power of immortality and is related to the Holy Grail and philosopher's stone. While it cannot be proven whether the stone came from the Sirius solar system or if humans had contact with Syrians in the distant past, scholars and mystics continue to study and research the stone to this day.

The power emanating from Shambhala, which Roerich and the mentors of the great white brotherhood and those of the Theosophical Society speak of, is said to be increasing the frequency of our planet. According to them, this power limited the second world war and was ultimately responsible for the fall of the Third Reich. It is believed that this transformative power will destroy all negative energies, such as greed and control, and accelerate the evolution of all life forms on Earth. Once its objective has been achieved, a planetary civilization based on love and equality may emerge and survive. The King of the world and his Chintamani Stone may finally announce their universal presence for all to see. The Dogon tribe in Africa claims to have been visited by beings from SIRIUS who shared knowledge about the grouping of three stars in the Sirius system and the moons surrounding certain planets in our solar system. This is seen as potential confirmation of the visit of carriers of the stone to Earth.

**The Dogon**

The existence of a group of people with a complex understanding of the universe, particularly the Syrian star, has been one of the most intriguing mysteries of ancient times. The Dogon tribe, who live in the Republic of Mali in West Africa, are believed to have possessed this knowledge for centuries. They arrived in Mali around 600 years ago and settled in the plateau of Bandiagara and the Homburi Mountains, about 1,500 kilometers from the Atlantic. The rocky terrain in this area is home to almost 450,000 Dogons, who have a unique approach to strangers and value peaceful conflict resolution due to their belief in the sanctity of life.

The Dogons' mythology is rich and complex, containing astronomical knowledge that is beyond explanation. This knowledge could not have been obtained by the tribe themselves, nor could it have been gained from any contact with beings from Earth. The enigma of their astronomical knowledge remains a mystery to science.

This village contains hidden knowledge about the solar system that has only recently become part of modern astronomy's collection. They knew that the moon is "dry and sterile" and that Jupiter, also known as "Dana tolo," has four large satellites. They were also aware of Saturn's rings and the elliptical orbits of planets around the Sun. This concept was only accepted by Western astronomy in the 17th century thanks to Kepler. They even described the Milky Way as a spiral galaxy made up of millions of conventional stars.

Despite their astronomical knowledge, the Dogon myths do not revolve around the solar system but instead focus on the Syrian star. This star, known as "Sigu tolo," is a first-magnitude star in the constellation of the greater Can. The Dogon's understanding of the brilliant Sirius is less significant than its invisible companion, Sirius B, a white dwarf star that Western astronomy did not discover until 1862. The Dogon refers to Sirius B as "Po tolo," which means "Star Digitaría" and "Po" means the smallest.

It is important to note that Sirius B ("Po tolo") has a magnitude of 8.7, making it invisible to the naked eye. Furthermore, the maximum separation between Sirius A and B is just 11 seconds of arc, which is hardly distinguishable by the human eye. In fact, the first modern visualization of Sirius B occurred in 1862 by Alvan Clark, using the largest telescope available at the time.

The Dogon myth tells of the "Star Digitaría" or Po tolo, which takes 50 light years to complete its orbit around Sigu tolo (Sirius A). Interestingly, astronomers estimate the same duration of 50,040 light years, with an impressively low estimation error of less than 0.08%. The myth also describes Po tolo (Sirius B) as white and composed of "sagala", an extremely dense and heavy metal that is believed to be the heaviest in the universe. This unique description fits that of a white dwarf. The Dogon also claims that Po tolo rotates on its axis in one year, which is likely to be accurate. According to them, Sirius B or Po tolo is the first star created by Amma and is considered the axis of the universe. The Dogon believe that the Sun and Sirius are twin stars with a common origin.

Furthermore, the Dogon are aware of other components of the system. They describe Sirius C as "Emme Ya", a much larger star than Digitaria but four times brighter. It is located in its orbit around Sigu tolo (Sirius A) at a distance of 50 light years, but further away. Its orbit of 50 light years coincides with the Festival of "Sigui," celebrated to commemorate the arrival of the Syrian gods. Modern astronomy estimates the calculations of this festival to be 50,040 light years. Emme has a satellite called "Nyan tolo," known as "the star of women," which serves as a guide. Until 1995, it was discovered that SIRIUS is a triple system. The "Shoemaker's star" is another additional member that is far removed from the other three and moves in the opposite direction around Sigui.

The Dogon depict the Syrian system as "the egg of the world," a precise orbital diagram in which Sirius A is one of the foci of the ellipse.

The Dogon people have a fascinating myth about the Sirius star system, which includes the "Star Digitaría" or Po tolo, a white dwarf composed of an extremely dense metal called "sagala." They also believe that Po tolo is the first star created by Amma and is considered the axis of the universe.

In addition, the Dogon are aware of other components of the system, including Sirius C, a much larger star than Digitaria, and its satellite Nyan tolo, known as "the star of women." Interestingly, the Dogon holds a ceremony of renewal of the world called "Sigui" every sixty light years, associated with the invisible Sirius B or Po tolo. They make masks with bird heads called "kanaga" for the occasion, which they carefully keep in protected shelters. These masks serve as physical proof of the Dogon's amazing knowledge about the SIRIUS star system, which dates back at least to 3200 light years, according to their traditions. According to Dogon legend, the Nummos, beings who came to Earth from the satellite of Emme, brought this astronomical knowledge with them. The Nummos are described as amphibious beings shaped more like fish than men, and they are referred to as "Masters of the water" and "Instructors." The Sumerian legend of the Oannes, which also describes fish-like beings who came out of the Red Sea, has disturbing parallels with the Dogon's Nummos.

**The belief of China**

There are ways to practice meditation and healing using the green stone "Moldavite" crystals. It's amazing how these crystals can substantially increase the flow of energy from the cosmos and the Earth's own field of energy to the individual. It's also interesting to know that the ability to heal oneself and others through the use and application of Qigong has increased greatly. Similarly, Reiki, the form of Japanese healing using the distribution of energy through the placement of the hands, has also shown similar results. I believe that increasing our sensitivity to higher frequencies, such as those presented by green stone (Moldavite) crystals, can definitely increase our awareness of what is possible with this system of healing.

**The sword of King Arthur-Excalibur**

According to English folklore, the hilt of the mythical sword Excalibur may have contained a jewel made of the green stone "Moldavite". There are several stories about how King Arthur acquired the sword, but the first version dates back to Geoffrey of Monmouth's "Historia of Regum Britanniae". It tells of Merlin forging Excalibur on the fairy island of Avalon and placing it in a stone next to a chapel in London. Arthur, who was originally the squire to his adoptive brother Cay, stumbled upon the sword and gave it to Cay after realizing it wasn't his brother's sword. When the sword was discovered to be stuck in the stone, Arthur was proclaimed as the rightful king.

## The philosopher's stone

The Moldavite, a crystal green stone, is often referred to as "The Philosopher Stone" due to its ability to turn thoughts into reality. It is believed that by using this stone, a student can find their way to the "Magnum Opus," the ultimate work of a master. This is because only the soul truly knows the path that leads to success.

## The Holy Grail

According to the Sacred Scriptures, Jesus was buried in a rock tomb owned by Joseph of Arimathea. With the assistance of Nicodemus Pharisee, a priest, Jesus was wrapped in fine linen and fragrant spices. Although little information is provided about Joseph of Arimathea in the Gospels and Scripture, it is believed that he was a wealthy man and a secret disciple of Jesus (John 19:38). Additionally, Luke suggests that José was a member of the Grand Council of the Sanhedrin, implying that he held a position of authority. It is said that Joseph of Arimathea, a "good and just man" (Luke 23:50), disagreed with the Sanhedrin's decision to sentence Jesus. According to Matthew (27:57-60) and Mark (15:43-5), José personally asked Pontius Pilate for the body of Jesus, indicating that he was powerful enough to secure an audience with the Roman Governor of Judea. Jewish tradition holds that it is the responsibility of the closest male relative to take care of the burial of the deceased, leading some to suggest that Joseph of Arimathea may have been Jesus' brother. However, Eastern tradition suggests that he was the uncle of the Virgin Mary.

There are various accounts of Joseph of Arimathea's life after the burial of Jesus. Some texts suggest that he was a friend of Pontius Pilate, while others claim that he was imprisoned by Jewish elders after the burial. According to one account, Jesus appeared to him while he was in prison and transported him to his house, where he was instructed to remain for forty days. Additionally, there is a tradition that Joseph of Arimathea took the young Jesus to England during his youth. While it is somewhat surprising that Joseph of Arimathea, a minor character in the New Testament, is associated with Great Britain, this tradition has been linked to Cornwall and Somerset. Some sources also suggest that Joseph of Arimathea fled Judea with a group that included the Apostle Philip, Lazarus, Mary Magdalene, and others. The group eventually arrived in Britain, where they were granted some lands by the local King AR virago in the "White Island."

There is a well-known myth about José de Arimathea and his supposed custodianship of the Holy Grail. As per the stories, the Holy Grail is associated with the cup that Jesus used during the last supper, and Joseph collected some of his blood in it during the Crucifixion.

The Holy Grail is a symbol of the lower world and man's bodily nature. Both of these are vessels of the living essence of the higher worlds. Such is the mystery of the redemptive blood, which overcomes death and spiritualizes the entire substance with its own immortality. For Christians, whose mystical faiths mainly emphasize "love," the Holy Grail symbolizes the heart that stirs the water of eternal life. Christians consider the search for the Holy Grail as a quest to find their true selves, which, once found, leads to the magnum opus.

Recently, the green stone "Moldavite" has been considered as a relic of the Holy Grail legend. In some accounts, the Grail is not a cup but rather a stone - an emerald that fell from the sky. In other stories, the Grail was a carved emerald cup. The similarity between the Grail stone and the green stone "Moldavite" is evident. All green stones were formerly referred to as "emeralds."

**Another story of the Holy Grail**

The Holy Chalice is said to be the cup that Jesus and his disciples drank from at the last supper. It measures 17 centimeters in height and is made of agate, dark red. According to tradition, it was taken from Jerusalem by St. Peter and used by the Popes for centuries to celebrate the Eucharist. The Cup was also the subject of many literary works, including poems like those written by Christian of Troyes and Wolfram of Eschenbach, which feature a vessel called the "Grail" or "Grail" that is connected to the Holy Chalice. The Holy Chalice is currently kept in the Cathedral of Valencia, where it has been since March 18, 1437.

In the year 258 or possibly 261, during the persecution of Emperor Valerian, Pope Sixto II gave relics, jewelry, and money to his deacon Lorenzo, who was also born in Huesca, Spain. Lorenzo was later martyred, but before his death, he sent the chalice of the Eucharist, along with a letter, to his hometown. The Cup remained in Huesca until the Muslim invasion when the Bishop of the city, Audeberto, left with the Holy Chalice in 713 to take refuge in the cave of Mount cloth where the hermit John de Atares lived. The monastery of San Juan de la Peña was later founded and developed in this place, and a core of hardworking men rushed to the reconquer against the Muslims. These epic characters were exploited by literary creation and are the origin or source of poems like those of Christian of Troyes and Wolfram of Eschenbach, with its hero Parceval or Parzival, which is subsequently Ricardo Wagner's Parsifal. In all these poems, there is a wonderful vessel called "Graal" or "Grail," whose relationship with the Holy Chalice is easy to understand.

The Holy Chalice's presence in San Juan de la Peña is documented in a document from December 14, 1134. On September 26, 1399, the chalice was moved to Zaragoza, at the request of the King of Aragon, Martin of Aragon - Martin the Humane. The text of delivery, which is preserved in Barcelona, notes that the Holy Chalice was sent from Rome with a letter from San Lorenzo. During the reign of Alfonso the Magnanimous, the relic was moved to Valencia. From March 18, 1437, it has been preserved in the Cathedral of that city, according to a document that refers to "Calyx that Jesus Christ consecrated blood the Jesus in the last supper."

# CHAPTER 6

## THE TRANSCENDENTAL GLASS

"The gem that fell from the sky"

The green stone "Moldavite" has gained popularity among users and scholars of metaphysics due to its supposed transformative and healing properties. Its scarcity has led to numerous stories about its effects on individuals' lives. Those who believe in metaphysics credit the green stone "Moldavite" with catalyzing personal evolution towards positive outcomes for oneself and others. The changes brought about by the crystal can be intense and rapid, with significant value for the individual. They may manifest in physical healing or the realization of dreams and hopes through heightened awareness or spiritual guidance. These manifestations can also impact one's professional career or personal relationships.

For those interested in using crystals for healing purposes, adding the green stone known as "Moldavite" to your collection may prove beneficial. This stone is reputed for its ability to promote quick healing and bring about powerful changes in one's life. The "Directory of Healing Crystals" by Cassandra Eason is a comprehensive guide to 150 crystals and gemstones and suggests that "Moldavite" may be useful in healing environmental problems. It is also believed to be an excellent option for curing illnesses that do not respond to conventional medical treatment.

This illustrated guide recommends keeping a glass green "Moldavite" stone with you, especially during times of solitude, as its healing properties can help to strengthen you and bring out your unique qualities. Crystal healing can also benefit children and aid in spiritual evolution.

The existence of "Moldavite" in human history dates back to prehistoric times, with evidence that it was considered a spiritual talisman in Eastern Europe during the Neolithic period. Excavations of the Venus of Willendorf site revealed a significant number of these stones, which were used as amulets for cures and successes in life. As a healing tool, "Moldavite" can promote harmonious relationships and help us align with the divine model proposed by the Supreme Being.

The green stone called "Moldavite" has been used for thousands of years in glass jewelry and crystal healing. However, due to its scarcity, its use was limited to select individuals like nobles and priests. This unique stone can be cut and polished into various geometric shapes, including pyramids, spheres, and gems like round, oval, triangular, or emerald. Its beauty is undeniable in any form. The shapes can help improve the focus and intensity of its healing power.

"Moldavite" is considered to be the most powerful tool in the mineral kingdom for the development of spirituality and knowledge. It is an excellent stone for meditation and is particularly suitable for the heart, third eye, and head chakras.

People sensitive to energy describe "Moldavite" as a stone with an extremely high vibration that can manifest itself in the form of heat, pulses, or other ways. Its high vibrations can remove blockages in the chakras and accelerate spiritual growth while facilitating better communication with spiritual guides. The stone's influence can be felt throughout the body, regardless of where it is placed.

Unlike other stones, "Moldavite" does not require energy cleaning. It can be recharged by exposure to sunlight and focused for a specific purpose or goal when cut into gem shapes or pyramids. Raw "Moldavite" is powerful, but faceted or pyramidal shapes enhance its focus.

## References

**Angelo Balladori**

On its website, Angelo Balladori describes a stone that belongs to the family of Tectitas. Tectitas may be meteoric, and they appear dark and slightly transparent when thin. However, the green stone "Moldavite" is a fully transparent bottle green. The stone is rare and expensive, and while scientists do not agree on its origin, they do agree on its age of around 15 million light years. The discovery of Moldavite's energy source is recent, and we are only at the start of understanding its potential. While it has recently become known to the general public, some ancient civilizations and knowledgeable beings, such as the priests and leaders of Egypt and Atlantis, were aware of its power.

Some theories suggest that the green stone "Moldavite" originated from space travelers or was a result of the destruction of Sodom and Gomorrah. The energy that Moldavite emits is unique and cannot be found in any other mineral. While quartz crystals can amplify energy, with Moldavite, cooperation with the stone is a different experience, and each individual must discover their path.

When holding the green stone "Moldavite" in the palm of your hand, you may feel continuous pulsations accompanied by heat or freshness. Your personal experience with the stone is entirely subjective; however, it can lead to reaching states of high spirituality. Moldavite can open your mind to unlimited visions, allowing you to understand your spiritual potential. It can accelerate the healing process and help identify possible psychological causes of disease.

If you are attracted to the green stone "Moldavite," you can seek it out and experience it for yourself. Your fruitful cooperation with this heavenly stone is just the beginning.

**Robert Simmons and Kathy Warner**

The book about Moldavite, the Starborn Stone of Transformation, explores the history and legends surrounding this unique blue-green gem. It is said to be a catalyst for healing and living life to the fullest, as well as a sacred talisman for spiritual awakening. Despite its long existence, it has gone unnoticed by many until now, at a time when we are reaching a critical mass and discovering its potential to unlock channels for personal growth in all areas of life. Moldavite has been regarded as a spiritual talisman throughout history and has even been linked to the legend of the Holy Grail. In modern times, it has become highly prized for its metaphysical properties, which can range from mild to overwhelming and can result in physical and spiritual cleansing and progress. Many people who come into contact with Moldavite report feeling its energy as heat or vibration, with sensations spreading throughout the body and sometimes leading to the opening of the heart chakra or other spiritual experiences. It is important to acclimate to the stone's energies and frequencies over time.

There is a stone called "Moldavite" that has special powers that can activate any of your chakras. It has a high intensity and frequency of vibration that resonates with the patterns of energy in a way that can intensify your spiritual vitality and accelerate your progress on the path towards higher goals. It is said to have the same effect as the legendary stone of the Grail.

The electromagnetic field accompanying the field of subtle energies is measurable, and with it, we can directly perceive the conditions of other people and the world. Hearts resonate from atoms to galaxies, from the individual soul to cosmic consciousness, and the heart is not only perceived but also changes the conditions. Through the heart, it is possible to modify reality and with that power comes responsibility for the maximum goodwill at all times. The green stone "Moldavite" offers the potential to help awaken the intelligence of the heart.

The green stone "Moldavite" is also a powerful aid to meditation and dream work. Placing a piece of the stone in front of you during these practices may lead to much clearer and better views of your internal experiences. It increases sensitivity and the ability to discern messages sent from higher realms. The stone can be a catalyst for self-healing, unblocking energy blockades, and opening meridians. Like the ancient, legendary agni mani, the green stone "Moldavite" is a talisman of spiritual awakening, transformation, and evolutionary growth.

Moldavite, a green stone often used in meditation and dream work, can also be fashioned into jewelry. Depending on the cut and faceting, the stone's energy can be enhanced. Pyramids, platonic solids, spheres, and tetrahedral stars are forms that can focus and expand the vibrations of the Moldavite. The most powerful cuts for jewelry are round brilliant, radiant type Octagon, oval, and triangular. The smooth and powerful round shape of the Moldavite allows for multidirectional flow of vibrations and a softness similar to that of spheres.

Moldavite is an ideal stone for activities requiring strength and power. It can be used on its own or in combination with other stones to amplify their effects. It can be added to various objects, such as sticks, bridles, templates, and networks, to increase their potency. Additionally, Moldavite can enhance and accelerate the beneficial effects of other stones, including quartz, amethyst, citrine, rose quartz, sugilite, charoite, lapis, larimar, rhodochrosite, aquamarine, heliodor, pietersite, smokey quartz, selenite, and many others. When paired with Herkimer "diamonds," the visionary experience can be intensified.

Moldavite is one of the 12 elements of synergy in stones, along with Danburite, Tanzanite, Azuztulite, Phenacite, Herderite, Tibetan tektites, Satyaloka quartz, Petalite, Brookite, Natrolite, and Scolecite. This combination is the most powerful for improving aesthetics and Moldavite works in harmony with each of these stones.

In the hypothetical scenario of being stranded on a deserted island with only one stone as an ally, Moldavite would be an excellent choice.

**Naisha Ahsian**

In the book "Letters from Allies of Crystal," Naisha Ahsian discusses the "Moldavite" gemstone and its transformative properties. This green gem fell to Earth over 14 million light years ago, arriving as a meteorite in the Bohemian Highlands. "Moldavite" is a cornerstone of transformation and its energy is immediately visible, producing clear and immediate effects of change.

The power of "Moldavite" is seen in the green beam it generates, which effectively renovates blocks in any chakra. It also strongly stimulates psychic senses and accelerates spiritual evolution, helping individuals find their own path. However, it is also a severe and drastic master, heralding violent changes in humanity's future. Anything or anyone that no longer serves a purpose will disappear, clearing the way for good and supreme well-being to arrive.

This transformational process is not easy, but relying on Universal will lead to a period of purification and spiritual development. "Moldavite" has an immediate impact on those who are attuned to its energy. Physical sensations may include heat, tingling, dizziness, and sometimes headaches. These symptoms are temporary and are a direct result of the gemstone's powerful force of purification on the chakras and energy systems of the body.

If you've been lucky enough to come across the "Moldavite," it could be a game-changer for you. Many people have reported incredible growth and transformation in their lives after encountering this powerful stone. It can affect your work relationships, personal life, skills, and creativity in ways you may not have thought possible.

If the "Moldavite" is working for you, be patient and trust that exciting things are on the horizon. Old relationships, jobs, and safety nets that no longer serve your ultimate path may disappear, leaving you completely transformed.

However, be aware that "Moldavite" is not always an easy ally. Its purging effects can put you in difficult and embarrassing situations, but this is all part of the process of change. The stone's high vibration can resonate with the universe's understanding and creation, leading to an increase in psychic phenomena and coincidences.

This is the perfect time to begin a new phase of spiritual development, with the "Moldavite" as your powerful guide and mentor. So embrace the change and trust in the process. Exciting things await!

**The Book of Stone**

In the book "The Book of Stone," the author discusses the power of the green stone known as "Moldavite." This stone represents transformation, cleansing, and change at all levels. It is known for its ability to activate the chakra system, stimulate the kundalini, and open channels for spiritual development. While it may seem intimidating, sometimes a "cosmic boot in the butt" is necessary to remove psychic debris and start on the path towards spiritual growth.

The green stone "Moldavite" can also reveal the limitations in one's life and spur them towards spiritual development. However, it is not for those who are addicted to safety and comfort. This stone demands willingness to confront and release what is holding you back. While it can be a powerful tool for communication and cosmic journeys, it should be used sparingly until one is acclimated to its frequency.

The green stone "Moldavite" teaches us to respect and harness our own power, and it can lead to profound spiritual experiences. Emotionally, it can bring up deep fears and shadows, but ultimately it shines a bright light on the depths of our being.

It is important to note that the green stone "Moldavite" should only be used with balanced and willing individuals. If one is frustrated and unable to identify the roots of their issues, it should not be used. It is best to approach this stone with an affirmation of openness to transformation and the manifestation of one's highest destiny.